P9-DWY-529

Better Homes and Gardens®

WOOD®
SCROLLSAW TECHNIQUES
AND PROJECTS YOU CAN MAKE

All of us at Meredith® Books are dedicated to giving you the information and ideas you need to create beautiful and useful woodworking projects. We guarantee your satisfaction with this book for as long as you own it. We also welcome your comments and suggestions. Please write us at Meredith® Books, RW-240, 1716 Locust St., Des Moines, IA 50309-3400.

© Copyright 1993 by Meredith Corporation, Des Moines, Iowa. All Rights Reserved. Printed in the United States of America.
First Edition. Printing Number and Year: 5 4   97 96 95 94
Library of Congress Catalog Card Number: 93-78103. ISBN: 0-696-00032-6.

A WOOD. BOOK
Published by Meredith. Books

MEREDITH. BOOKS
President, Book Group: Joseph J. Ward
Vice President and Editorial Director: Elizabeth P. Rice
Executive Editor: Connie Schrader
Art Director: Ernest Shelton
Prepress Production Manager: Randall Yontz

WOOD. MAGAZINE
President, Magazine Group: William T. Kerr
Editor: Larry Clayton

SCROLLSAW TECHNIQUES AND PROJECTS YOU CAN MAKE
Produced by Roundtable Press, Inc.
Directors: Susan E. Meyer, Marsha Melnick
Senior Editor: Marisa Bulzone
Managing Editor: Ross L. Horowitz
Graphic Designer: Leah Lococo
Design Assistants: Leslie Goldman, Betty Lew
Art Assistant: Marianna Canelo Francis
Proofreader: Amy Handy

For Meredith. Books
Editorial Project Manager/Assistant Art Director: Tom Wegner
Contributing How-To Editors: Marlen Kemmet, Beverly Rivers,
    Charles E. Sommers
Contributing Techniques Editor: Bill Krier
Contributing Tool Editor: Larry Johnston
Contributing Outline Editor: David A. Kirchner

Special thanks to Khristy Benoit

Meredith Corporation Corporate Officers:
Chairman of the Executive Committee: E. T. Meredith III
Chairman of the Board, President and Chief Executive Officer:
    Jack D. Rehm
Group Presidents: Joseph J. Ward, Books; William T. Kerr, Magazines;
    Philip A. Jones, Broadcasting; Allen L. Sabbag, Real Estate
Vice Presidents: Leo R. Armatis, Corporate Relations;
    Thomas G. Fisher, General Counsel and Secretary;
    Larry D. Hartsook, Finance; Michael A. Sell, Treasurer;
    Kathleen J. Zehr, Controller and Assistant Secretary

On the front cover: Nature in the Round, pages 60–61
On the back cover: Trains, Planes & Automobiles, pages 56–59 (left);
    Winter Wonderland, pages 44–46 (bottom right)

SCROLLSAW TIPS AND TECHNIQUES

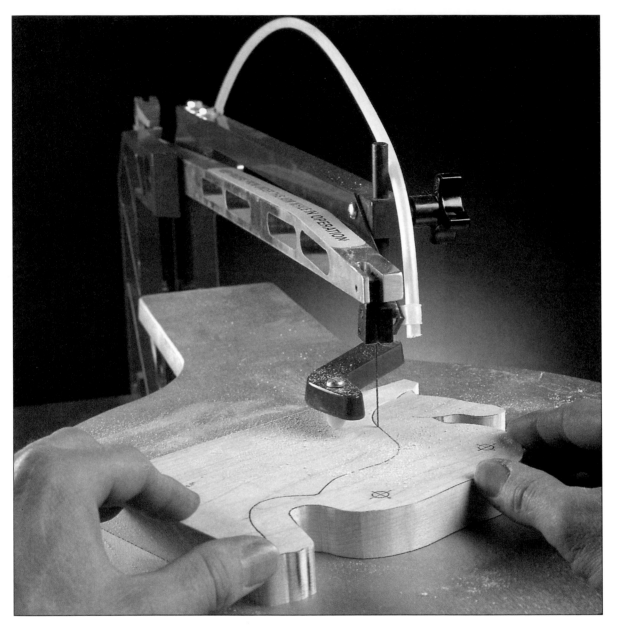

Here are practical tips and professional techniques to help you with your scrollsaw work. You'll find information on buying equipment and copying patterns—and we've even included six great scrollsaw projects to get you started.

THE WOODWORKER'S GUIDE TO SCROLLSAW BLADES

A while ago, I bought a new scrollsaw. And, a couple of weeks later I had exhausted the supply of blades provided with the saw. Instead of just spending a few bucks at the local hardware store for the brand carried there, I did some research into the topic. Let me tell you, poking my nose into the scrollsaw-blade business provided me with a real education. Read on and I'll fill you in.

—Bill Krier
Products/Techniques Editor

Pin- or plain-end blades: It depends on your saw

Those of us who already own a scrollsaw really have no options when buying new blades. Most saws generally accept only one type—either pin- or plain-end blades. Both have advantages.

As shown *below*, a small pin at each end of the blade serves as a holding device in the pin-end types. Although slightly more expensive (about 7 cents more per blade), pin-end blades quickly slide into place for hassle-free mounting. But, I discovered that even though plain-end blades require a little more work to clamp into position, nearly all serious scrollsawers use them. And, Chuck Olson of the Olson Saw Co. tells me plain-end blades outsell pinned blades by

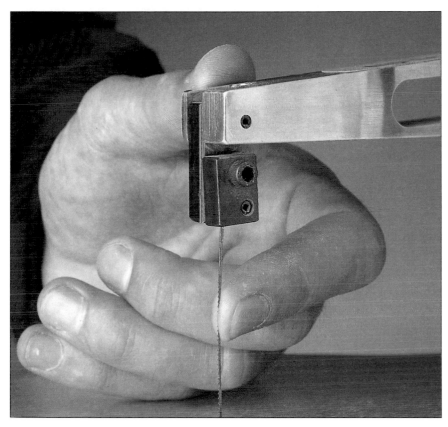

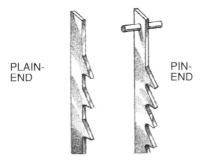

PLAIN-END   PIN-END

about 20 to 1. "You can buy plain-end blades in a much greater variety of sizes and tooth configurations," Olson told me. "And because pin-end blades have to be wider to accept the pin, they're not available in the thin sizes necessary for intricate work."

Choose a coarseness to match the job

Ron King, who travels the country demonstrating scrollsaws for Advanced Machinery Imports (AMI), has plenty of advice on buying scrollsaw blades. Of all the pearls of wisdom he passed on to me, this one really cut to the core of the matter: "Select the coarsest blade that gives a cut that's satis-

factorily smooth for your job." Coarse blades, because of their extra width, help you cut a straighter line. Fine blades, on the other hand, cut more smoothly than coarse ones, but they also cut more slowly and break more often. So, it pays to test coarser blades first, then turn to finer blades as you look for the ideal type for your project.

As you can see by the chart on *page 6*, plain-end blades have universal numbers, with the high-numbered blades being the coarsest. Various suppliers assign different model numbers to pin-type blades, but the same width, thickness, and teeth-per-inch guidelines apply to choosing the right pinned blade.

continued

What blades do the pros use? To find out, I asked Gene Douglas, co-owner of Marlow Woodcuts in Americus, Kansas. His family operation cranks out more than 5,000 intricately scrollsawed pieces every year and goes through more than 2,000 blades in the process. Gene wouldn't reveal his source, as he considers that a trade secret, but he did tell me what *type* of blade he favors. For ⅟₁₆" walnut plywood with a poplar center, the Marlow scroll-sawers clamp No. 2/0 scrollsaw blades into their machines, and use No. 5 standard blades when sawing ⁵⁄₁₆" solid walnut.

What you need to know about tooth patterns

As you can see from the illustration *above right,* scrollsaw blades come in five different tooth patterns. Here are a few tips on each:

•**Standard.** Sometimes referred to as a skip-tooth or fretsaw blade, these kerf-cutters easily outsell all other types. The gullet between each tooth helps clear away wood chips and cool the blade. In my hands-on testing, this blade cut faster and smoother than any other blade in ¾" stock. Available in plain-end only.

•**Double tooth.** Currently, only AMI imports these blades, but because of their rising popularity the Olson Saw Company is also considering manufacturing them. "These are AMI's hottest-selling blades," Ron said. In the *WOOD®* magazine shop, double-tooth blades produced less chip-out than the other blades in materials less than ⅛" thick.

•**Scrollsaw.** Most often found in coarser sizes, especially in pin-end blades, these stiff blades work best in rigid-arm scrollsaws. Although not recommended for smooth or intricate cuts, the wide (.250") versions of this blade work well for straight cuts such as rips. Available with plain and pinned ends.

•**Reversed.** This new blade from the Olson Saw Company has five or six teeth at the bottom of the blade that point upward. Why? The reversed teeth reduce splintering on

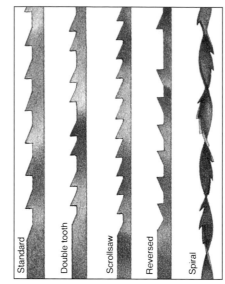

Standard · Double tooth · Scrollsaw · Reversed · Spiral

the bottomside of the workpiece. Available in only a few coarser sizes of plain-end blades.

•**Spiral.** These twisted scrollsaw blades leave a wide kerf. But, because they cut in all directions you don't have to rotate the workpiece for curved cuts. And, they work well for bevel cuts. Plain-end only.

A few more blade-buying guidelines

•For metal cutting, buy a jewelers blade. Available in up to 20 universal sizes, these plain-end, hard-ened blades have the same tooth pattern as scrollsaw blades.

•If you plan to buy a scrollsaw, keep in mind that you'll find the widest array of blades in the 5" length. Although the majority of saws accept this size, some "hobby" machines take 2¾" blades.

•Don't forget that the quality of your scrollsaw may have a bearing on your blade purchase. As Ron King told me, "If I'm using a less-expensive Sears or other Taiwanese-made saw, to avoid breakage I have to buy a thicker and wider blade than if I'm working with a Delta, RBI, Hegner, or other high-quality saw."

•And yes, it's nearly impossible to tell one size scrollsaw blade from another. So, you need a storage system such as the one we designed (see *opposite*).

Information Guide

For more information and catalogs, contact:

• Advanced Machinery Imports, P.O. Box 312, New Castle, DE 19720, or call 302-322-2226.

• Olson Saw Co., 16 Stony Hill Road, Bethel, CT 06801, or call 203-792-8622.

UNIVERSAL NUMBER	WIDTH	THICKNESS	TEETH PER INCH	APPLICATIONS
— CHOICES, CHOICES: CUTTING THROUGH THE MAZE OF BLADES (standard, skip-tooth, plain-end blades listed)				
2/0	.015–.022	.010	28–30	Extremely intricate sawing in veneers, plastics, hard rubber, and pearl up to ³⁄₃₂" thick
0	.024	.011	25	
1	.026	.011–.012	23–25	
2	.028–.029	.012–.013	20–23	Tight radius work in hardwoods to ½" thick, soft-woods to ¾", and plastics to ¼"
3	.032	.013–.014	18–20	
4	.035	.014–.015	15–18	
5	.038–.039	.015–.016	12½–16½	Tight radius work in hardwoods to ¾", softwoods to 1", and plastics to ½"
6	.041–.043	.016–.017	12½–15	
7	.045	.017–.018	11½–14	Hardwoods to 1", softwoods to 1½", plastics to ½"
8	.047–.049	.017–.018	11½–14	
9	.053	.018–.019	11½–14	
10	.056–.057	.019–.020	11–12½	Hardwoods to 1½", softwoods to 2", plastics to ¾"
11	.059–.063	.019–.020	9½–12½	
12	.062	.024	9½	

SCROLLSAW BLADE ORGANIZER

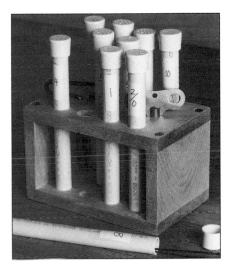

Scrollsawers know that laying their hands on the right blade can be tricky and time-consuming, especially if these tiny cutting tools get mixed together. This handy little organizer ends those hassles in a hurry by separating and storing your blades. And all you need to build it is a small amount of scrap stock and some ½"-diameter (⅝" O.D.) CPVC pipe and caps.

For still more convenience, drill a few extra holes in the rack top to hold your scrollsaw tools. Consider labeling the tubes for easy reference. You can hang the unit on a wall or set it on a flat surface near your scrollsaw.

EXPLODED VIEW

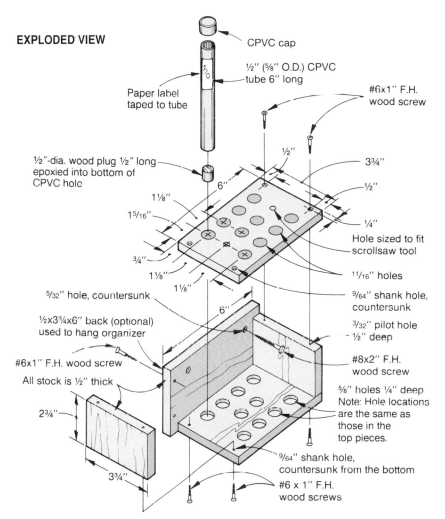

CPVC cap

½" (⅝" O.D.) CPVC tube 6" long

Paper label taped to tube

#6x1" F.H. wood screw

½"-dia. wood plug ½" long epoxied into bottom of CPVC hole

6"

½"

3¾"

½"

¼"

Hole sized to fit scrollsaw tool

1⅛"

1⁵⁄₁₆"

¾"

1⅛"

1⅛"

¹¹⁄₁₆" holes

⁹⁄₆₄" shank hole, countersunk

⁵⁄₃₂" hole, countersunk

6"

³⁄₃₂" pilot hole ½" deep

½x3¾x6" back (optional) used to hang organizer

#6x1" F.H. wood screw

All stock is ½" thick

#8x2" F.H. wood screw

⅝" holes ¼" deep
Note: Hole locations are the same as those in the top pieces.

2¾"

⁹⁄₆₄" shank hole, countersunk from the bottom

3¾"

#6 x 1" F.H. wood screws

7

TEN TIPS FOR IMPROVING YOUR SCROLLWORK

Next time you attend a woodworking show, check out the scrollsaw booths. You'll meet demonstrators who can scroll rings around most woodworkers. What do they know that you may not? Just a few tricks, such as the tips on these pages.

2. Scrollsaws come with a variety of blade clamps, but whatever the style, make sure the blade sits straight in the clamps as shown at *bottom*.

With that accomplished, set the blade for the correct tension. Remember that you can tension a wide blade more than a narrow

blade and that overtightening will lead to excessive blade breakage. On the other hand, a loose blade will flex sideways and backwards.

3. Time flies when you're having fun with a scrollsaw, so adjust the machine's table to a comfortable working height (near elbow level for most people). You'll also find it helpful to sit on a chair or stool.

4. As shown *below,* scrollsaw blades will flex under even slight feed pressure, so you need to occasionally slow down the feed rate and allow the blade to straighten itself. If you don't, you may cut a kerf that's not perpendicular to the table or bowed slightly. While cutting thick or dense stock, you may need to pause every ½" or so.

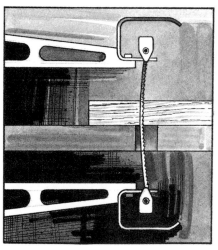

1. Because of the rapid up-down strokes of its arms, a scrollsaw vibrates excessively when not securely fastened to a stand. If your machine doesn't have such a perch, bolt the scrollsaw to a sturdy surface. If you need to store your scrollsaw between uses, clamp it down.

If you can't clamp or bolt down the machine, try placing a thin foam pad, such as a carpet pad, underneath the machine as shown *above.*

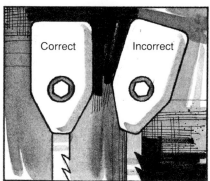

Correct   Incorrect

5. We've found that paper patterns are easier to see than patterns transferred directly to the wood surface by carbon paper or other means. Adhere the paper to the workpiece with adhesive spray, rubber cement, or double-faced tape.

6. A dustblower helps you see exactly where you're cutting, but for it to be effective, you must reposition it for each stock thick-

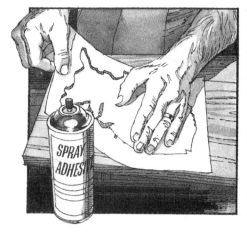

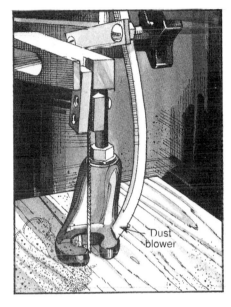

ness. Most blowers put out a small volume of air, so place the hose tip no more than ½" from the cutting action.

7. As you move the workpiece into the blade, start and exit the cut at a sharp point on the pattern rather than along a smooth line as shown *below left*. Otherwise, your lines will have small "humps" where you enter and exit the cut.

8. Because many of us have become accustomed to following layout lines on a bandsaw—a machine that doesn't allow cutting extremely tight curves—we're not used to rotating a workpiece as shown *above*. Experienced scrollers often spin their workpieces in full circles to precisely follow tight twists and turns. When carefully executed, this maneuver may look tricky, but it just requires some practice.

To train yourself, draw some squiggly lines on a scrap piece and see how closely you can follow your markings. Soon you'll be spinning with the best of 'em.

9. Sometimes, you can't spin your way through extremely tight spots such as the narrow corner shown *below center*. To smoothly execute this maneuver, first cut all the way into the corner, then back up the blade for Cut 2. Now you have enough room to turn the blade around and make the exit cut.

10. We hear from a lot of readers who have problems cutting thick, hard stock with a scrollsaw. If that sounds like you, try a wider, skip-tooth blade. Go slow and clear away cutting debris by backing the blade out of the cut often.

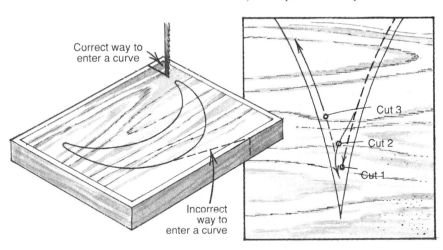

Correct way to enter a curve

Incorrect way to enter a curve

Cut 3
Cut 2
Cut 1

PANTOGRAPH DRAWING BOARD

Books, magazines, photos, and even coloring and comic books offer endless pattern sources for wood-workers. Unfortunately, though, they're seldom the right size for your particular project. With a commercially available panto-graph and our drawing board, enlarging and reducing patterns become as simple as tracing an outline. The money you save on purchasing patterns will quickly pay for the entire project.

Start by making the drawing board

1. Cut a piece of ¾" plywood (we used birch) to 24x40" for the drawing board (A).

2. To band the plywood drawing board, rip two ¼x25"-long walnut strips from the edge of a ¾"-thick board for the ends (B). Rip two ¼x41"-long walnut strips for the top and bottom (C). Glue and clamp the end strips to the drawing board, checking that the surfaces are flush. After the glue dries, remove the clamps, and trim and sand the ends of the banding flush with the edges of the drawing board. Repeat for the top and bottom banding strips.

3. Sand the top and bottom edges of the banding flush with the top and bottom of the drawing board (we used a palm sander).

Here's how to mount the pantograph pivot shoe

Note: The Lutz pantograph listed in the Buying Guide and shown in the photo above right *comes with an instruction brochure. Read the instructions to assemble the unit and to locate the parts described in this article. The instructions also give detailed information on operating the pantograph when enlarging or reducing patterns.*

1. Using the dimensions on the Exploded View drawing, *opposite,*

With the eagle pattern centered in the 2:1 ratio rectangle and the blank paper in the copy area, we're doubling the size of the pattern onto the blank paper.

mark the location of the center of the pivot shoe. Using the holes in the pivot shoe as guides, drill a pair of ³⁄₃₂" pilot holes in the drawing board for mounting the pivot shoe.

2. Fasten the pivot shoe to the drawing board with a pair of #6x½" roundhead wood screws.

Marking the enlarge-ment rectangles

1. Mark the copy-area rectangle on the drawing board where dimen-sioned on the Exploded View draw-ing. (We darkened our lines with a permanent felt-tip marker and a straightedge.)

2. To mark the 4:1-ratio rectangle (¼ the size of the copy-area rec-tangle), set the ratio screws in holes

Follow the outline of the copy-area rectangle with the tracing point to mark the 4:1 ratio rectangle on the drawing board. Darken lines with a felt-tip marker.

PANTAGRAPH DRAWING BOARD

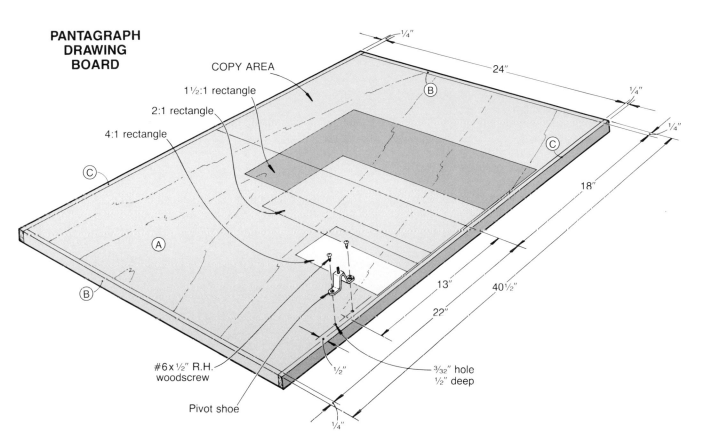

COPY AREA

1½:1 rectangle

2:1 rectangle

4:1 rectangle

¼"

24"

¼"

¼"

18"

13"

40½"

22"

½"

³⁄₃₂" hole
½" deep

#6 x ½" R.H.
woodscrew

Pivot shoe

¼"

number 4 in the pantograph bars. Then, exchange the position of the tracing point and lead holder as they come from the supplier. Now, trace the outline of the copy-area rectangle with the tracing point. As you do this, the lead will draw the small rectangle on the drawing board as shown on the photo at *left. (Note that we clamped a framing square flush with the edges of the copy-area rectangle to ensure straight perimeter lines on the 4:1 ratio rectangle.)*

3. Repeat this same process with the ratio screws in holes number 2 for the 2:1 ratio rectangle, and in holes number 1½ to mark the 1½:1 ratio rectangle. (We selected the ratios most commonly used, although you may want to draw in other ratios as well. Also, when enlarging, we have found the 4:1 setting about as large as we can go before the drawn enlargement starts getting sloppy.)

4. Apply several coats of finish (we used polyurethane for a hard, durable finish).

How to use the pantograph

Begin by exchanging the position of the tracing point and lead holder. Now, to enlarge a pattern 4 times the original size, for example, tape the original pattern, centered, in the 4:1 ratio rectangle and tape the blank paper, centered, in the copy-area rectangle. Fasten the ratio screws in holes number 4 in the pantograph bars. Now, trace the original pattern with the tracing point and the lead will draw the enlarged pattern on the paper.

To reduce patterns, place the original pattern, centered, in the copy-area rectangle. Tape blank paper in the desired ratio rectangle. Reverse the positions of the tracing point and lead holder. Following the outline and detail lines with the tracing point, trace the original pattern.

Buying Guide

•**Pantograph.** Constructed from aluminum, this device offers 25 enlarging ratios of 1⅛ to 8 times and reducing ratios of ⅞ to ⅛. Includes instructions and replaceable lead points. Catalog No. 78147. For current prices, contact Leichtung Workshops, 4944 Commerce Parkway, Cleveland, OH 44128, or call 800-321-6840.

Project Tool List
Tablesaw
Portable drill
  ³⁄₃₂" bit
Finishing sander

Note: *We built the project with the tools listed. You may be able to substitute other tools or equipment for listed items you don't have. Additional common hand tools and clamps may be required to complete the project.*

REPRODUCING PROJECT PATTERNS

You won't find "gridphobia" listed in Webster's. Medical encyclopedias completely ignore it. But woodworkers feel gridphobia's grip when faced with enlarging a pattern. Their minds freeze at the thought of transposition. Yet, know-how immediately cures the ailment. With photographic technology, **it happens in a flash. Even by hand, pattern enlargement becomes child's play.**

Due to space limitations, most carving patterns or designs published in magazines, books, and project plans *must* be printed at a reduced size—for you to enlarge. Many woodworkers cringe at the idea—finding pattern line inter-sections, placing dots on squares, penciling and erasing—and pass such projects by.

Enlarging isn't difficult, however, and special machines and tools make it even easier. Besides, learning the techniques of pattern enlargement and duplication unlocks unlimited sources of designs—ones gridphobiacs will never see.

HOW TO TRANSPOSE A PATTERN

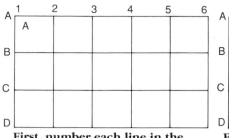

First, number each line in the vertical row. Then, place a letter on each horizontal line.

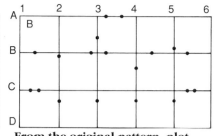

From the original pattern, plot every point where line intersects a square with a dot on your pattern.

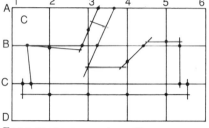

For a more accurate pattern, connect all the straight lines first.

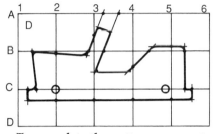

To complete the pattern, connect the dots that represent curves.

TRACING AND TRANSFERRING A HALF-PATTERN

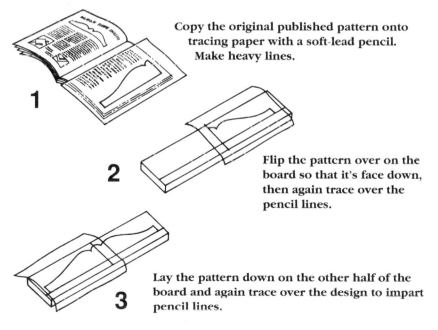

1 Copy the original published pattern onto tracing paper with a soft-lead pencil. Make heavy lines.

2 Flip the pattern over on the board so that it's face down, then again trace over the pencil lines.

3 Lay the pattern down on the other half of the board and again trace over the design to impart pencil lines.

Play "follow the dots" with hand enlargement

In publishing, graphic designers reproduce *grids* to illustrate patterns. Those requiring enlargement include the statement *"Each square equals 1""* (or ½" and so forth). This notation means that no matter what size grid squares you see in the drawing, you *must* enlarge squares for your full-size pattern to the size indicated.

To use the hand-enlargement method called *transposing*, you'll need *cross-section graph paper* (the kind with heavier lines marking off each square inch and subdivisions of four or more inner squares), a ruler, an eraser, and a soft-lead pencil. If graph paper isn't available at art, mechanical-drawing, school-supply stores or variety retailers, make your own by dividing plain paper into the specified-size squares.

Begin by marking off on your grid paper the same number of squares as indicated on the pattern grid. Next, number each vertical line in the pattern from left to right and letter each horizontal line from the top down, as in Drawing A, *top left*. Then, mark the corresponding squares on your graph paper the same way.

Start your pattern enlargement by finding a square on your graph paper that matches the same square on the original. Mark the graph paper grid square with a pencil dot in the same comparative place where a design line intersects a grid line on the original, as shown in Drawing B, *above left*. Work only one square at a time. Continue to neighboring squares, marking each in the same way where a design line intersects a grid line.

To avoid discovering any mistakes too late, mark only part of the design, then stop and join the dots with a pencil line. Try to reproduce the original contours as accurately as possible, as in Drawing C, *above left*. For more precision, draw all straight lines first; then add the curved and angled lines, shown in Drawing D, *above left*. Once you have transposed part of the design, finish

continued

REPRODUCING PROJECT PATTERNS
continued

marking the rest of the squares and join those dots in the same way.

Sometimes, as when a pattern repeats itself on the other side of a center line, you'll only have a *half-pattern* to use. To duplicate a full-size half-pattern, copy the original with a soft-lead pencil on tracing paper. Next, flip your traced pattern over and place it pencil-lines-down onto one half of the board. After aligning the pattern for position, go over the pattern lines with your pencil to imprint it on the board. Then, flop the pattern onto the second half of the board and again retrace the pattern to imprint it, as shown in Step 3 in the tracing drawings on the *previous page*. This method proves faster than copying with carbon paper and doesn't mark up the original pattern.

Push the button and let a machine do the work

In this technological age, a photocopier with enlargement capability enlarges a pattern faster and more accurately than transposing. (Not all copiers enlarge, and even some of those that do may be a little inaccurate, so always check your results with a ruler.)

To find out the enlargement percentage you'll need, measure the grid size of the pattern you want to copy. For example, if the magazine's pattern grid measures ½" and the scale calls for 1", you'll need an enlargement twice the size, or 200 percent. A pocket calculator simplifies the mathematics—just divide the number representing the full-size scale by the grid size of the original magazine pattern, then hit the percent (%) key.

Photocopiers have limitations. The ideal photocopier for enlarging patterns—sometimes owned by architectural firms—has the ability to enlarge by 1-percent increments. Some may have only a few sizes of enlargement (or reduction) from which to choose,

A mechanical tool to toy with

With a device called a *pantograph,* you can enlarge (or reduce) patterns at your desktop or workbench. Looking very much like the expandable, protective gate used to keep toddlers from tumbling down a stairwell, a pantograph consists of an arrangement of hinged arms. After you adjust the device for the enlargement needed, you outline the original pattern with the stylus, or tracing end. While you trace the lines with the stylus, the pantograph's pencil end draws the enlargement. It's as simple as that.

Although pantographs usually have an enlargement capability up to 8:1, you'll get sharper reproduction if you stick to a limit of 4:1 (400 percent). If you don't, you'll find yourself working in a tiny area with the stylus while the pantograph's fully extended pencil arm flaps about. To enlarge greater than 4:1, do it in two steps. That is, for an 8:1 enlargement, use the pantograph to first make a 4:1 enlargement. Then, again enlarge the pattern 2:1. (See a related article on *page 10* about a pantograph board you can build.)

In setting up the pantograph on your worktable or drawing board, be sure to affix the original pattern and the copy sheet close enough to each other so that the arms won't spread excessively (see photo, *below)*. Be sure, also, to tighten all the pantograph fittings. Any looseness creates wobbly, floppy arms and inaccurate tracing.

You can buy a pantograph at art supply stores. They are made in wood or metal and are available at a reasonable price.

To avoid wobble, which results in inaccurate reproduction, don't spread the pantograph's arms too wide. Tighten all fittings, too.

or have a limit on how large the enlargement can be. With the latter, you can still make a full-size pattern by enlarging it in two steps.

For instance, the photocopier's enlargement limit might be 150 percent and you need a 200-percent enlargement. So, first make an enlargement of the original to the 150-percent limit. Then, using a calculator, divide your desired size of 200 by your enlargement limit of 150 percent (200 divided by 150). Your answer will be 133 percent.

Next, set the machine to copy at 133 percent and enlarge the pattern you already made at 150 percent. Your final pattern will be 200 percent larger than the original.

Patterns by projection—just like school

A few machines enable you to quickly and accurately enlarge a pattern. Typically, they're not found at home, but available (for a fee) from libraries, schools, and audio-visual rental companies.

An *opaque projector* accepts flat, horizontal artwork and projects it onto a vertical surface, such as a screen or a wall. Enlarge or reduce a pattern by taping a graph-paper grid to the wall. Place the original pattern in the projector, and then line up its projected squares on your wall-mounted paper grid. Keep moving the projector back and forth to the wall until the grids line up. When they do, pencil in the projected lines.

An *overhead projector* receives transparent material in the form of a clear acetate sheet, and projects the image onto a screen or wall. An overhead projector operates in the same way as an opaque projector, except that you must trace the lines of the original pattern onto the clear acetate with a nonsmearing, felt-tip marking pen before projection.

The printing, publishing, and advertising industries enlarge artwork with huge cameras. The same method works perfectly for enlarging patterns. For a few dollars you can purchase a correctly sized *reproduction stat* ("stat"), a black-and-white photo print of the original that provides accurate detail. You simply

request that the print be made to the exact size you want. Check the Yellow Pages under "Photostatic Copy Service" or "Photo Copying." Sometimes, fast-service print shops offer reproduction stats, too.

Finding proportions with dividers

Proportioning dividers, available at drafting-supply stores, enable you to accurately enlarge even a tiny section of a pattern, such as a fractional line or other detail. However, this tool won't draw the segment for you.

Dividers perform solely as a measuring device. First, you measure the length of a line on the original pattern with the points on one end of the dividers. By setting the enlargement size, the points on the opposite end will automatically extend themselves to the enlarged size. To transfer the measurement to the enlargement, flip ends of the dividers (see photos, *below*). With proportioning dividers, you can transfer minute details.

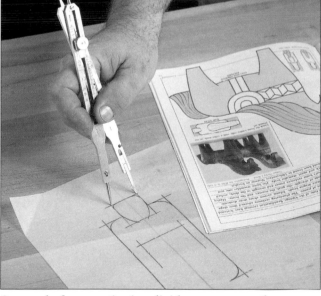

One end of proportioning dividers measures the dimension of a detail on the original.

The other end translates the original dimension to the exact scale you choose for the reproduction.

SIX FUN-TO-DO SCROLLSAW TECHNIQUES

Are you tired of cranking out the same old cookie-pattern cutouts on your scrollsaw? We are. So we decided to have some real fun with our saw and turn out some scrollsawn gifts that would make our friends and relatives stand up and take notice. In the process, we came up with six neat scrollsaw techniques. We hope they'll spark your imagination—for holiday gifts, and projects throughout the year round.

Ladies and gentlemen, choose your blades

The chart at *right* lists the best blade sizes for the techniques shown in this article, *provided* you use the stock thicknesses suggested in the chart and in the text.

If you use thicker material, select a wider, thicker blade with fewer teeth per inch. For thinner material, use a narrower, thinner blade with more teeth. Likewise, if you're cutting an intricate pattern with lots of sharp curves, use a narrower blade than is ordinarily recommended for the thickness of stock you're cutting. The reverse is true if you're cutting straight lines, or patterns with gentle curves.

Note: Some of the photos in this article show the saw's hold-down foot elevated so you can better see what's going on. But we recommend you keep the foot in its proper position—down against the stock—while making all cuts. On most scrollsaws, the foot not only holds the stock firmly against the table while you're cutting, but also serves as a blade guard to protect your fingers from the blade.

Technique	Blade*		
	W	**T**	**TPI**
1. Wooden Puzzle	.037–.040	.015–.016	13–14
2. Scrollsaw Puzzle	.029–.032	.012–.013	18–20
3. Relief Technique ¾"–1" stock	.053–063	.018–.019	9.5–11.5
4. Inlay Technique ¼"–½" total thickness	.037–.043	.015–.016	12–14
5. Wood Sculpture ¼"–⅜" stock ½"–¾" stock	.037–.040 .043–.053	.015–.016 .016–.018	13–14 11.5–12
6. Stack Cutting ⅜"–¼" total thickness	.029–.032	.012–.013	18–20

*W–width, T–thickness, TPI–teeth per inch

*Note: We chose the blade sizes based on their ability to make tight, intricate cuts in the stock thicknesses indicated. Use wider blades for simple patterns and straight-line cutting.

1. Scrollsawing wooden puzzles for tiny tots

Brightly colored, durable wooden puzzles fascinate young, growing minds. If you're making the puzzle for a preschooler, choose a pattern your little gift recipient will easily recognize, with pieces large enough not to be swallowed.

• With a pen or pencil, divide the pattern into puzzle segments—eight to 10 easily identifiable pieces should do for most puzzles.

• Cut a square or rectangular piece of ¼" birch plywood large enough to provide a ½" to 1" margin around the pattern. (This piece forms the puzzle parts and frame.) Then, from ⅛" birch plywood or hardboard, cut a piece the same size as the frame for the frame backing.

• Center the pattern on the frame, then attach it with artist's spray-mount adhesive. Drill a hole in the frame just large enough to thread the scrollsaw blade through it, insert the blade, and cut out the overall pattern shape, as shown in the photo, *upper right*. Now, detach the blade from the saw arm and remove the frame and cut-out pattern piece.

• Reattach the blade. Cut the pattern piece into individual puzzle parts, as shown in the photo, *upper middle*. Remove the paper pattern from the individual pieces.

• Glue the backing piece to the backside of the frame. After the glue dries, sand the frame

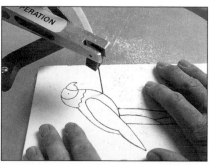

Mount your paper pattern on the wooden puzzle frame. Then, cut around the puzzle outline.

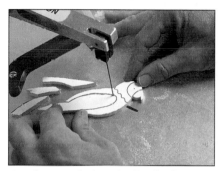

Cut the puzzle into individual parts, sand the parts smooth, and paint them bright colors.

and puzzle pieces with 220-grit sandpaper, rounding over the edges slightly.

• Use nontoxic paints to paint each puzzle piece a different color, and a clear nontoxic finish for the frame.

2. How to make scrollsaw puzzles for kids of all ages

Sure, most people do call them jigsaw puzzles. But we call them

scrollsaw puzzles because you can't beat a scrollsaw for cranking out a lot of them in a hurry. Here's how to do it:

• Cut out a suitable print, poster, or magazine photo, and glue it to a backing of ⅛" hardboard. (We found that an all-purpose spray adhesive, such as Touch 'n Stick or 3M Super 77, works well.)

• With a straightedge and grease pencil (we used a white one), draw light grid lines on the puzzle face to indicate the size and number of puzzle pieces you want.

• Cut the pieces freehand, using the grid lines as a general guide. Cut each puzzle piece so it interlocks with the adjoining ones, as shown in the sketch, *below*. Make all of the lengthwise cuts first. Then, flip the puzzle upside down, and tape the strips together, as shown in the photo, *below*. Now, flip the puzzle back over and make all the crosswise cuts.

• Remove the grease-pencil marks by wiping *lightly* with a soft cloth dampened with lighter fluid. Don't rub too hard or the fluid

continued

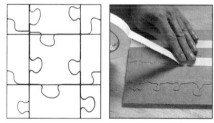

Glue the picture to the puzzle, mark grid lines, and make all lengthwise cuts. Then, flip the puzzle over and tape the cut lines together with masking tape.

The tape holds the puzzle together while you make crosswise cuts to separate the individual pieces.

SIX FUN-TO-DO SCROLLSAW TECHNIQUES
continued

Cut out the oval on the scrollsaw, staying slightly outside the line. Then, remove the waste with a disk sander.

may also remove the ink from the picture.

3. Give your next project a bit of relief

Need a gift for your Aunt Martha? She'll surely make room on the wall for a lovely scrollsawn relief plaque like the dove pictured *above.*

• Select the material for your workpiece blank, then cut it to size. (We used ¾" Honduras mahogany for the oval dove plaque.)

• Attach your pattern to the workpiece with artist's spray-mount adhesive. Then, drill a blade-threading hole or holes in an inconspicuous part of the pattern, such as an inside corner. (The dove plaque requires a separate threading hole for each of the six cutouts.)

• Thread the blade into the workpiece, then cut each pattern piece. Next, cut the background to the desired shape. (We cut the oval plaque slightly oversize, then sanded it to finish size with a disk sander, as shown *above right.)*

• Sand a slight roundover on the top edges of the pattern pieces and the inside edge of the background. Then, sand all the parts smooth.

Glue the cut-out pieces to the frame from the back side. Use cotton swabs to spread the glue evenly.

• Place the background *upside down* on a piece of waxed paper, and prop it up with ¼" spacer blocks, as shown in the photo, *above.* Insert the cut-out parts into the background, then run a bead of woodworker's glue around each piece.

• After the glue dries, attach a saw-toothed hanger to the back of the plaque, then apply a clear finish.

Note: *On our dove plaque, the dove projects from the background. If you want your pattern recessed into the background, prop up the cut-out parts, instead.*

4. How to make glove-tight inlays

Use this bevel-cutting technique to make solid-wood inlays for boxtops, wall plaques, and other projects To do it, your scrollsaw must have a tilting table. (We used ⅛" walnut and maple for the unicorn inlay. We then glued the inlaid piece to the top of an unfinished walnut box purchased at a local craft supply store.)

• Choose two contrasting woods of the same thickness for the inlay and background pieces. Cut the pieces large enough for your pattern plus at least 3" at one end for making

To determine the exact table angle for making inlays, make test cuts in the waste portion of your workpiece. The plug from the top piece should fit snugly into the piece underneath as it does in the test cut at right.

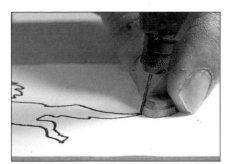

Use the last test plug you made as a guide to drill the blade-threading hole at the correct angle.

test cuts when you set the tilt angle of the saw table.

• Start with the saw table set at an angle between 8° and 12° (see note *below*). Tape the workpieces together with double-faced tape, then cut out a "test plug" in the margin area (see photo *opposite, bottom right*).

Note: If you've tilted your table to the left, as we did in the photo, on page 18, rotate the stock counterclockwise into the blade to cut out the test plugs and pattern. If you've tilted your table to the right, rotate the stock clockwise into the blade. If you cut in the wrong direction, you'll get the

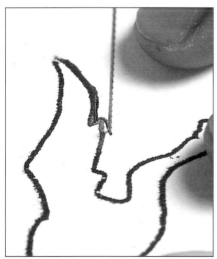

When cutting outside curves, the blade may drift outside the line. To compensate, slow the feed rate and apply pressure against the downhill side of the blade.

reverse—the cut-out portion of the bottom piece will fit neatly into the top piece!

Now, push the plug from the inlay (top) piece into the hole cut out of the background piece. If the plug doesn't fit snugly into the hole, reset the table angle and try again. (Notice in the photo that the middle plug dropped too far into the background piece. To compensate for this, we increased the table angle a few degrees to get the tight fit shown *below left*.) You may have to repeat this process several times before you get a tight, flush fit. Once you do, save the last plug you cut to serve as a guide block for drilling your blade-threading hole.

• Attach your pattern to the workpiece with spray-mount adhesive. Then, use the last plug you cut in Step 2 as a guide block to drill your blade-threading hole at the correct angle, as shown in the photo *above left*.

• Thread the blade through the hole and cut out the pattern.

Note: When cutting out patterns on a tilted table, gravity sometimes works against you. We found that the blade tends to drift toward the uphill side of the line when turning outside corners, as shown in the photo at left. You can compensate by slowing down the feed rate when making outside turns and applying slight pressure against the downhill side of the blade.

• Apply a thin coat of woodworker's glue around the edges of the inlay. Press-fit it into the background. Wipe off glue squeeze-out.

• After the glue has dried, fill any imperfections with colored wood putty or glue mixed with sanding dust. Then, use a sanding block with 220-grit sandpaper to sand the entire surface. Now, incorporate the inlaid piece into your project.

5. Wood sculpting made easy

Here's a good way for you noncarvers to make a classy wood "sculpture" with your scrollsaw and sanding machine.

• Select a segmented pattern and cut it into its various components. Then, choose the type and thickness of wood you want for each pattern component and the background. (We made our sailboat sculpture from varying thicknesses of maple, walnut, and Honduras mahogany against a background of ¼" oak.)

• Mount the pattern parts on the workpieces with spray-mount adhesive, as shown in the photo on *page 20, top*. If the pattern includes long, narrow pieces, lay them out parallel to the wood grain. Also, keep grain direction in mind while attaching the other pattern pieces for the most attractive looking parts. Cut out the parts on your scrollsaw.

• Sand the face side of each workpiece to the desired shape. (In the photo, *page 20, right,* we're shaping the boat hull on a *continued*

SIX FUN-TO-DO SCROLLSAW TECHNIQUES
continued

Mount the pattern pieces on stock of different thicknesses and kinds of wood, then cut out the individual parts on your scrollsaw.

stationary belt sander.) Sand only the area of each piece that will project above the background surface. Smooth the parts with 220-grit sandpaper.

• On a piece of waxed paper, glue the parts together with quick-set epoxy. (Use small brads to hold the pieces in position, as shown in the photo *above right*.) Then, touch up the finished assembly with 220-grit sandpaper.

• Cut the background piece to size, position the assembled sculpture on the face side, and trace the sculpture outline onto it.

• Drill a blade-threading hole into the background piece, install the blade, and saw the cutout for the sculpture. Now, remove the background piece from the saw and smooth it with 220-grit sandpaper.

We found our stationary belt sander an excellent tool for quickly sculpting larger parts. You also can shape the parts on a disk sander or drum sander. Shape smaller parts by hand sanding.

• Insert the sculpture into the face side of the background, using a few pieces of masking tape to hold it in place, if necessary. Now, turn the work-piece face-down and spread quick-set epoxy into the joints between the sculpture and background. Before the epoxy sets, flip the piece back over and lay it, glued side down, on waxed paper.

• After the glue dries, remove the waxed paper and sand the back smooth (we used a belt sander). Touch up any rough spots on the face side of the sculpture with 220-grit sandpaper. Apply a clear finish of your choice to both sides of the finished sculpture.

6. Stack 'em up, cut 'em out, mix 'n' match

Stack cutting enables you to make several cutouts from one pattern. If you use contrasting woods, you can interchange the pieces, and glue them back together so no two cutouts will be alike. Use ⅛" stock for small items, ¼" stock for larger ones.

• From each type of wood you want to use, cut a piece slightly larger than your pattern. (We used ⅛" walnut, maple, and Honduras mahogany for the rocking horses shown *opposite, top.*) Stick the pieces together, using double-faced tape.

• Cut out your pattern and mount it on the stock with spray-mount adhesive. (If you want to reuse the pattern, make several photocopies.)

• Cut out the pieces as shown in the photo *opposite, center.*

Note: To keep tiny parts from falling through the blade slot in the saw table, make a zero-clearance table top, *as shown in the photo,* opposite, bottom left. *Cut a piece of ¼" plywood the same size as the saw table and clamp it to the table. Then, drill a small hole for the blade and thread it through the plywood top.*

• Separate the stacked parts and remove the tape. Then, arrange the parts on a piece of waxed paper and interchange the parts to make figures of interesting, contrasting colors as we did with the three rocking horse examples *opposite, top.* If you have trouble separating the small pieces, dip them in a pan of lacquer thinner, then gently pry them apart.

• Edge glue the pieces together with quick-set epoxy, using ½" brads to hold them in position,

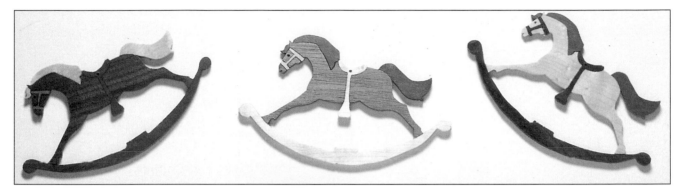

as shown in the photo, *bottom right*. (With our horses, we first glued the tiny head pieces together to form a larger piece, then glued this piece onto the rest of the figure.)

• After the glue dries, sand the decorations with 150- and 220-grit sandpaper to remove excess glue. Apply a clear finish. For tree ornaments, drill a ¹⁄₁₆" hole in each one, then insert a string or wire.

Note: *We chose these blade sizes based on their ability to make tight, intricate cuts in the stock thicknesses indicated. Use wider blades for simple patterns and straight-line cutting.*

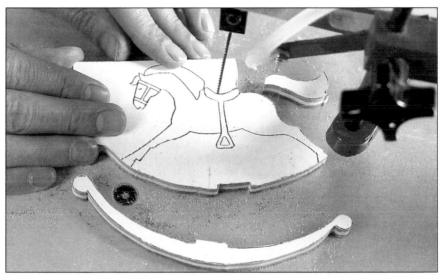

Double-faced tape holds the stacked pieces together while you cut out the ornament parts.

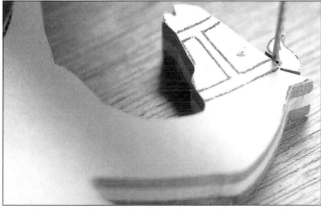

Attach an auxiliary top of ¼" plywood to the scrollsaw table and drill a small hole for the blade. This keeps tiny pieces from falling through the table's blade slot.

Lay the parts on a piece of waxed paper and glue them together with a quick-set epoxy. Use small brads to help hold the pieces together until the glue dries.

SIGN-MAKING MADE EASY

A sampling of some of the artwork in the "Graphic Symbols" clip art book (one in a series of Graphic Source books from Graphic Products Corporation).

Sure, you can make relief signs by routing or carving, but once you team up a bandsaw with a scrollsaw to do them, you may never return to your old ways. While this simplest-of-all third approach saves time, its greatest reward lies in the crisp, well-defined relief lines that give your signs increased readability and a sharp look. Here's how to do it.

First, lay out your sign

After deciding on your sign's message, sit down and draw a rough sketch of what you want it to look like. When sizing the sign, keep in mind the maximum cutting height of your bandsaw for resawing operations. As you'll see later, signs higher than the maximum cutting height of your bandsaw require additional steps as described on *page 25*.

No matter what sign shape you choose, it should have a frame that surrounds the letters and extends to the sign's perimeter. You can make the frame into a circle, rectangle, or free-form—any shape that complements your message. In the sign shown *above* and *left,* we chose an oval frame for added interest.

You say you don't have access to an alphabet? Not to worry. We've included letters and numbers; use and reuse them as much as you like. You can enlarge them on many photocopiers, but we advise against making them any smaller. Why? The scrollsawing technique shown in this article requires bevel cuts that you'll find difficult or impossible to make with smaller letters. If you would like to try another alphabet, visit an art-supply store and check out its stock of stencil or transfer (rub-on) letters.

You also may want to incorporate into your sign a graphic element such as those shown *opposite*. If one of these symbols doesn't fit the theme of your sign, you can purchase clip-art books—again, at an art-supply store—that contain hundreds of other symbols. We've found the "Graphic Symbols" clip-art book shown *below* especially useful. It has silhouetted images depicting animals, plants, foods, tools, toys, hobbies, holidays, vehicles, sports, and much more. To obtain your copy, see the Buying Guide on *page 27*.

To make a pattern, begin with a blank sheet of paper as big as your sign. With a pencil draw guidelines on the paper that help you align the letter bottoms. If you go with the alphabet shown here, photocopy and cut out each letter or number that you'll need. Then, tape

FULL-SIZED ALPHABET PATTERNS
● Scrollsaw blade start hole (use 1/16" drill bit)

Aa

or paste the characters on your guidelines, paying attention to spacing the letters or numbers in a pleasing way. (If using transfer or stencil letters, you'll need to rub-on or trace the characters along the guidelines.) Finally, photocopy, cut out, position, and affix any graphic elements. After completing your design, photocopy it to make a cutting pattern for the next steps.

Choose the perfect piece of stock

For our sign we chose teak because of its weather resistance and attractive grain pattern. The prominent grain lines also help you in assembling the sign later, but less-figured woods such as Honduras mahogany work well, too. Other species to keep in mind for outdoor signs include cedar, redwood, white oak, and cypress. Whatever species you decide on, remove any planer marks and smooth the face side with a succession of abrasives before moving on to the following steps.

Note: For the best appearance, make your sign from one piece of stock, rather than edge-gluing several pieces to gain the necessary width. Wide signs (over 10") may cup, so we advise you make these from several edge-joined pieces. For outdoor signs, be sure to use a water-resistant glue such as slow-set epoxy or Franklin Titebond II. If you must glue up the stock, do so only after you read the next section on preparing your stock.

The techniques and letter sizes suggested here work well with ¾" stock. If you use thinner material, *continued*

SIGN-MAKING MADE EASY
continued

you'll lessen the relief effect. If you choose stock thicker than ¾", you'll need to proportionally increase the minimum size of the letters and numbers. For example, with 1½" stock, enlarge the alphabet shown here to twice its size. Otherwise, you may have difficulty making some of the beveled scrollsaw cuts in tight areas.

Get into the thick of it by resawing your stock

If the height of your sign does not exceed the maximum resawing capacity of your bandsaw, attach a copy of the pattern to the face side of the workpiece (rubber cement works well). Then, mark a resaw line along the top edge of the workpiece that's centered on the stock's thickness. Mark the word "top" on the side of the resaw line opposite the pattern. Then, with a ¼"-or-wider blade with 6 teeth per inch, resaw the workpiece as shown *right*. To do this accurately, we suggest you build the simple bandsaw resawing jig shown in the photo *right* and illustrated *below*.

Position and clamp the resawing jig to your bandsaw table so that you can guide the workpiece along the pointed edge of the jig. Be careful to align the jig parallel with the blade and workpiece. To safely resaw the sign stock, push it through the blade until you come to within about 3" of the end of the workpiece. Then, pull both resawn pieces (called the *pattern piece* and

A simple resawing jig helps you follow your marked line. Note that we marked "top" on the background piece to aid in assembling the sign later.

background piece) completely through the blade.

If the height of your sign exceeds the maximum resawing capacity of your bandsaw, as shown in the drawing *opposite, lower left,* rip your workpiece into widths that fit underneath the saw's upper guide assembly. Or, make the sign from several workpieces, none of which exceed the maximum resawing capacity or your bandsaw. (For best results, pay careful attention to matching the color and grain of the workpieces.)

In any event, mark the faceside of each workpiece. Then, number both faces of each of the workpieces in their glued-up order to help you keep them straight later.

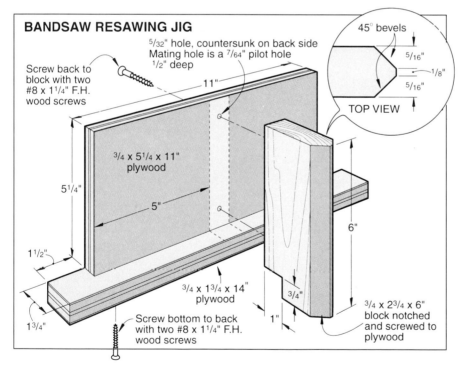

BANDSAW RESAWING JIG

5/32" hole, countersunk on back side
Mating hole is a 7/64" pilot hole
½" deep

Screw back to block with two #8 x 1¼" F.H. wood screws

11"

45° bevels

5/16"
1/8"
5/16"

TOP VIEW

¾ x 5¼ x 11" plywood

5¼"

5"

6"

1½"

1¾"

¾ x 1¾ x 14" plywood

Screw bottom to back with two #8 x 1¼" F.H. wood screws

¾"

1"

¾ x 2¾ x 6" block notched and screwed to plywood

Tilt your scrollsaw table 10° to the left or right and keep the waste side of the cut on the downhill side of the blade.

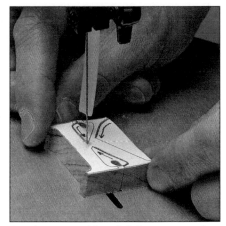

Cut just one side of tight corners (as shown by the arrows), and then tilt the table and cut the other side.

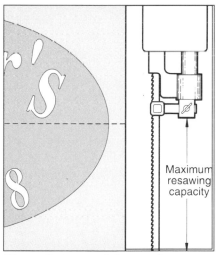

Pieces that exceed the maximum cutting height of your bandsaw should be ripped to a width that can be resawn. After resawing, edge-glue the pieces back together.

Maximum resawing capacity

Resaw each piece as described *opposite*. Then, assemble the resawn pieces in the correct order and edge-glue them, being careful to make your glue-ups as flat as possible. Now, affix your pattern to the face side of your pattern piece.

Now, for best results, bevel-cut your sign

To add visual interest to your sign, make all of your scrollsaw cuts at a 10° bevel. (We used a No. 5 blade—one that's .038"–.039" wide, .015"–.016" thick, and has 12½–16½ teeth per inch.) To do this, you need to tilt your scrollsaw table 10° to the left or right. Then, as you cut along the pattern lines, rotate the workpiece to keep the waste side of the cut on the low "downhill" side of the blade as shown

left. (The letter, symbol, or other piece that will be a part of your sign stays on the high "uphill" side of the blade.) This technique can be tricky until you get used to it, so practice on scrap before tackling your sign. In no time you'll develop a knack for this procedure.

Because of the bevel, you will find that you can't turn tight corners as you normally can with a scrollsaw. So, when cutting into an inside corner, you need to first cut along one side and stop when you reach the corner's point as shown *above*. Then, turn off the machine, back the blade out of the cut, tilt the table 10° the other direction, and cut the opposite side of the corner to complete the cut. To save time, make cuts along one side of each inside corner in your workpiece before tilting the table. If your table tilts in only one direction, see the boxed information on *page 26*.

It's time to put all of the pieces back together again

With your parts cut from the pattern piece, you now need to affix them to the background piece.

continued

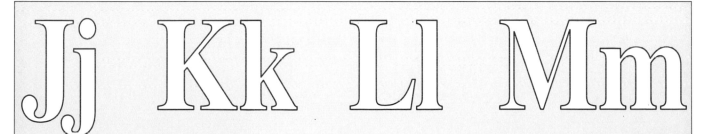

Jj Kk Ll Mm

SIGN-MAKING MADE EASY

continued

What if your scrollsaw table tilts only one way?

Even if your scrollsaw's table doesn't tilt both left and right, you can still make beveled cuts along both sides of a corner with a simple 10° tilted auxiliary table shown *below.* You can fasten this jig to your scrollsaw table with double-faced tape so it tilts to either the left or right. In the photo *below left,* we're using this auxiliary table to complete the cuts made in the photo on *page 25, top right.*

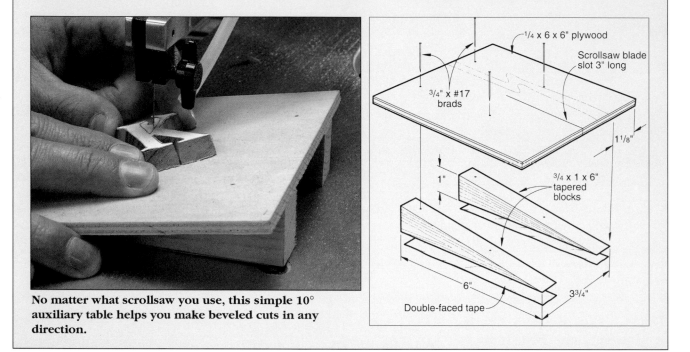

No matter what scrollsaw you use, this simple 10° auxiliary table helps you make beveled cuts in any direction.

First, glue the piece that frames your letters and symbols to the background piece. Affix this frame in the same position it was in when you resawed it from the background earlier.

Now, set the background piece on a bench, with the frame facing up and the edge marked "top" facing away from you. Place all of the cutouts onto the resawn surface in the positions they occupied before being cut out. For help, use a copy of the pattern as a guide. If the stock has visible grain lines, use these to help you position the figures, too.

Next, hold down each character with a nail set and mark its place with an X-ACTO knife as shown in the photo on *page 22.* Use the same knife to individually lift each character off the background so that you can apply glue as shown *opposite, top.* We prefer gap-filling instant glues or epoxies. Use a slow-set epoxy for outdoor signs,

and avoid excessive squeezeout around the base of the characters when you set them in position.

To bring out the natural beauty in these signs, we applied a coat of Watco Natural Danish Oil Finish. For outdoor signs, apply a protective finish such as Thompson's Water Seal. No matter what finish you choose, apply equal amounts to the front *and* back of the sign to reduce warpage.

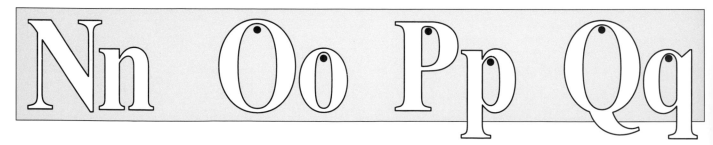

When applying adhesive, use an X-ACTO knife to pick your characters off the resawn surface. Orient the knife blade with the grain to avoid marring the workpiece.

Here's what happens if you reverse the pattern

For a different look altogether, you may want to try cutting away the characters in your sign and leaving the background, as shown at *right*. If you prefer this sign style, leave your scrollsaw table at 90° to the blade. We found that tilting the table yielded no noticeable visual effect.

Buying Guide
• **Graphic Source Clip Art Library.** Available at art-supply stores nationwide. For more information contact Graphic Products Corporation, 1480 S. Wolf Rd., Wheeling, IL 60090, or call 708-537-9300.

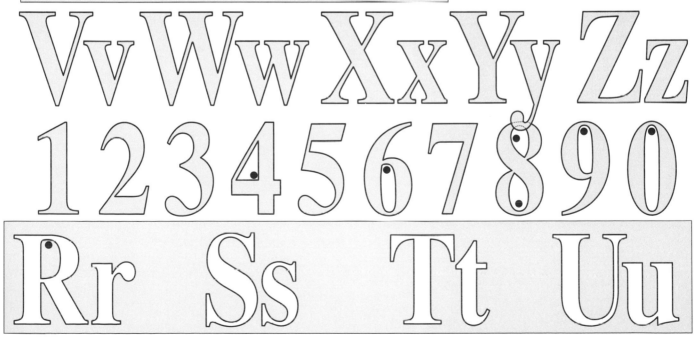

SCROLLSAW GIFTS
FOR THE HOME

This group of projects will add a touch of craftsmanship to your home decor. From wall hangings to picture frames to decorative items for the holiday table, the results of your labors are sure to please yourself or a lucky recipient.

DUCK UNDER GLASS

Seeking a distinctive-looking project? Search no more. We sandwiched this spirited wildlife scene between two contrasting sheets of glass, matted it with oak, and then rimmed the project with a complementary walnut frame. Hang this scene on the wall, or add a pair of walnut feet to stand it on a shelf.

Note: If you plan to hang the project on the wall, add a picture-hanging wire to the back. For a freestanding unit, add the feet.

You'll need some thin stock for this project. You can either resaw or plane thicker stock to size.

Let's start with the frame

1. Have one piece of ⅛" gray-tinted glass and one piece of ⅛" clear glass cut to 10¾x11¾". For a good fit later, double-check that both pieces of glass square up and measure the same size.

2. From ⅛" walnut (we planed thicker stock), cut two pieces of stock to 1⅛" wide by 26" long for the exterior frame pieces.

3. Using the Foot and Frame detail accompanying the Exploded View drawing for reference, cut a pair of ⅛" kerfs ¼" deep along the length of each frame strip. Check the fit of the glass in the grooves

and widen the grooves slightly if necessary. Sand the two strips.

4. For the matlike inner frame, rip and crosscut two pieces of ¼" stock to 1½x24". (We used oak.)

5. Miter-cut the inner frame pieces to length, and position them on one of the glass panels; the outside edges of the pieces should be ¼" in from the outside edges of the glass panel. Trim if necessary.

6. Spread waxed paper on a flat surface. Apply woodworkers' glue to the mating mitered ends of the inner frame pieces. Assemble the frame on the waxed paper. Drive nails into the work surface next to the frame members to hold the pieces firmly together. Check that the surfaces remain flush. Later, sand the frame.

Time to fire up the scrollsaw

1. Make three photocopies of the pattern. Using one of the

continued

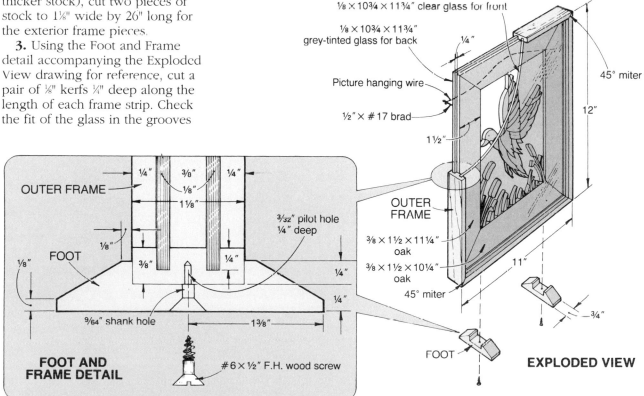

FOOT AND FRAME DETAIL

EXPLODED VIEW

DUCK UNDER GLASS
continued

FULL-SIZED PATTERN

COLOR KEY

Raw umber

Parchment

Light green

Yellow oxide

Phthalocyanine green

White

White

White

White

White

photocopies and spray adhesive, adhere the paper pattern to ¼" Baltic birch plywood.

2. Scrollsaw the pieces to shape (we used a No. 2 blade). Peel off the paper pattern from the scrollsawed pieces. If the paper pattern resists removal from the wood, add a splash of lacquer thinner to dissolve the spray adhesive. Position the scrollsawed pieces on the second photocopied pattern.

3. With 220-grit sandpaper, lightly sand the cut edges of each piece.

4. Brush paint on each piece using the opening photograph as a guide. (We used acrylic paints.)

Fasten the pieces to the glass, and add the frame

1. Thoroughly clean both faces of each piece of glass.

2. Tape the third full-sized pattern to a flat piece of stock. Center the gray-tinted glass over the paper pattern and tape the glass to the work surface.

3. Using clear silicone sealant, center and adhere the inner frame to the glass.

4. Add a dab of silicone to all painted pieces, and adhere them to the glass, positioning them directly over the paper pattern as shown in the photo *above right*. (We used tweezers to accurately locate the smaller pieces.)

5. Remove the glass and attached parts from the work surface. Place the piece of clear glass on the front of the colored pieces. Set the two pieces of glass aside.

6. Add the finish to the inner surfaces of each outer frame piece.

7. Fit the outer frame pieces onto the glass. Being careful not to get glue or dust inside the framework, apply glue to the mitered corners of the frame and clamp them. (We held the pieces together with strapping tape until the glue dried.) Check for square.

8. Sand the mitered joints flush, mask the glass on the front and back of the assembly, and add the finish to the rest of the frame.

Place a fine bead of silicone sealant on the back side of each piece, and then adhere the pieces to the glass directly above the outline on the photocopied pattern.

9. To hang the project, partially drive two ½"×#17 brads into the outside frame pieces, positioning the brads 1¼" from the top edge and ³⁄₃₂" in from the outside edge. Wrap and tie a 12½" length of picture-hanging wire around the brads, and then finish tapping the brads into the frame.

For a freestanding unit, add the feet

1. Transfer the foot pattern twice to a piece of ¾×1½×12" walnut. Cut the dadoes where shown on the drawing *below,* and then cut the feet to shape.

2. Drill and countersink a hole through the bottom center of each

foot. Sand the feet and add the finish.

3. Position the feet on the bottom of the assembly 1⅜" in from the outside edges. Use the holes in the feet as guides to drill mating holes in the bottom outer frame member. Screw the feet in place.

Supplies

#6×½" flathead wood screws, ⅛" glass, clear silicone sealant, acrylic paints, clear finish, two ½"×#17 brads, and picture-hanging wire.

Project Tool List

Tablesaw
    Dado blade or dado set
Scrollsaw
Portable drill or drill press
    Bits: ³⁄₃₂", ⁹⁄₆₄"
Finishing sander

Note: *We built the project with the tools listed. You may be able to substitute other tools or equipment for listed items you don't have. Additional common hand tools and clamps may be required to complete the project.*

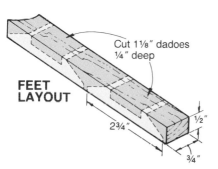

FEET LAYOUT

Cut 1⅛" dadoes ¼" deep

2¾"

½"

¾"

HIGH-FLYING PHOTO FRAME

Symbolizing peace and love, the doves and hearts on our scrollsawed frame make it just right for displaying a youngster's photo. But, don't you think it would be a nice addition to a child's room, too, with a photo of mom and dad or the grandparents in the place of honor?

Note: Start with two 6" squares of ¼"-thick stock to make this frame. Plane or resaw thicker stock. The small inside cuts call for a fine, plain-end scrollsaw blade. (We used a No. 5 blade, .037X.015" with 14 teeth per inch.)

1. Make two photocopies of the full-sized pattern *opposite*. Attach one to each piece of stock with spray adhesive or rubber cement. Place the patterns on the stock (we used ash) so that the grain runs crosswise on each piece. This way, the thinnest section of the frame—the picture surround on the frontpiece—won't be as likely to break off when you saw it. Drill ¹⁄₁₆" blade start holes and the holes for the stand where shown on the pattern.

2. Cut out the hearts on the frontpiece first, and then the larger opening, following the broken pattern line. Don't make the rectangular frame around the picture opening too narrow—it must overlap the inside edges of the backpiece cutout to form a lip. Cut slightly on the waste side of the pattern line. Do not cut the outside to shape yet. On the back piece, follow the solid lines to cut out the birds and the picture opening. Again, do not cut the outside to shape.

3. Peel the paper pattern from the backpiece. Clean off any remaining adhesive (we used lacquer thinner), and then lay the frontpiece on the backpiece. Make an even margin between the large frontpiece opening and the cutout birds. Then, sparingly apply woodworker's glue to the back side of the frontpiece and clamp the two pieces together, double-checking the positioning.

4. After the glue has dried, saw around the outside pattern line. Remove the pattern from the frame, clean off the adhesive, and sand. Chamfer the front and back edges with a piloted chamfering bit in a table-mounted router.

5. Now, attach the stand where shown (we made ours from coathanger wire). Apply a clear spray-on finish from several angles to cover all surfaces. Insert the photograph, holding it in place with tight-fitting cardboard or a few drops of hotmelt glue.

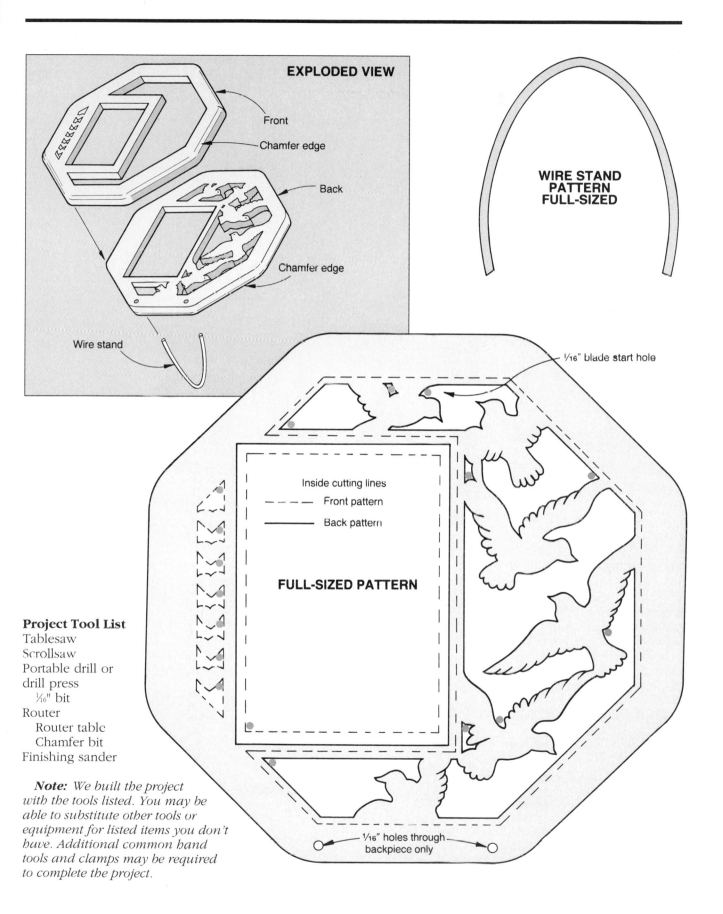

EXPLODED VIEW

Front

Chamfer edge

Back

Chamfer edge

Wire stand

WIRE STAND PATTERN FULL-SIZED

1/16" blade start hole

Inside cutting lines

- - - Front pattern

——— Back pattern

FULL-SIZED PATTERN

Project Tool List
Tablesaw
Scrollsaw
Portable drill or
drill press
  1/16" bit
Router
  Router table
  Chamfer bit
Finishing sander

Note: *We built the project with the tools listed. You may be able to substitute other tools or equipment for listed items you don't have. Additional common hand tools and clamps may be required to complete the project.*

1/16" holes through backpiece only

STANDING-TALL BLOCKS BOX

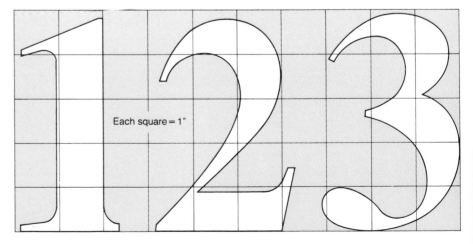

There comes a time in every child's life when being just a few inches taller would open up great new possibilities. Whether it's getting a drink of water or turning off the light, many kids wobble through this stage balancing on chairs or other precarious perches. Here's a better plan: let them stand tall on this sturdy box of blocks.

1. Rip and crosscut the front and back (A), ends (B), and top and bottom (C) to the dimensions shown in the Bill of Materials. Cut the trim strips (D and E) and eight 5¼" squares for the numbers and letters from ⅛" plywood or tempered hardboard. Refer to the Exploded View drawing, *opposite,* and then assemble the sides and ends with screws and woodworker's glue.

2. Place the front and back between the ends. Attach the top and bottom, and then sand the box smooth and the corners flush. Now, add the trim strips. Place a long strip (D) on one end face, flush with the top edge of the box. Cut or sand the ends flush with the

front and back of the box, and attach the strip with woodworker's glue and brads (we used ½"×#18 brads).

3. Place another long strip along the bottom. Then, complete the square frame on the end by fitting short trim strips (E) vertically

Each square = 1″

between the horizontal pieces. Keep the edges flush at the front and back of the box.

4. Attach strips to the other end, then to the front and back, and lastly to the top. Leave a ⅛" space where shown on the top, front, and back to create the look of two separate blocks.

5. Enlarge the letter and numeral patterns *below* with gridded paper or an enlarging photocopier. Enlarge at 129 percent, again at 129 percent, and then at 121 percent. Separate the patterns, and then affix one to each of six of the squares with spray adhesive.

6. Because you need a total of eight figures, stack-cut two copies of the "A" and "B." To do this, adhere one of the remaining squares to the back of the piece with the "A" pattern and the other to the piece with the "B" pattern using double-faced tape. Drill blade start holes where indicated on the "A" and "B" patterns. Then, cut out the letters and numerals, starting with the inside cuts. (We drilled ¼" blade start holes and used a .110x.022" blade with 15 teeth per inch.) Center a letter or numeral in each square, and attach with glue and brads.

7. Fill the brad holes and trim-strip joints as necessary. Sand, rounding over the corners slightly, and apply white latex primer.

8. Paint the step stool with white latex enamel, and accent the raised faces with brightly colored enamels. Apply two coats of clear acrylic

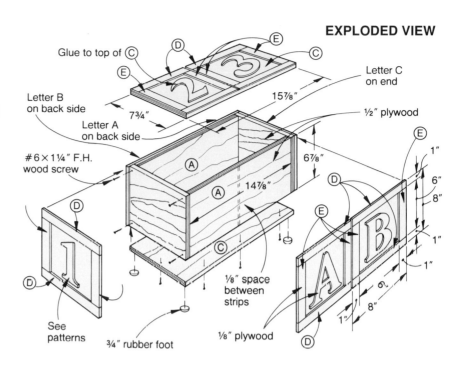

EXPLODED VIEW

Glue to top of Ⓒ
Letter B on back side
Letter A on back side
#6×1¼" F.H. wood screw
See patterns
¾" rubber foot
Letter C on end
15⅞"
½" plywood
6⅞"
14⅞"
⅛" space between strips
⅛" plywood
7¾"
1"
6"
8"
1"
1"
6"
8"
1"

after the paint dries. Attach ¾" rubber feet to the bottom to prevent skidding.

Project Tool List
Tablesaw
Scrollsaw
Portable drill or drill press
    ¼" bit
Finishing sander

Note: We built the project with the tools listed. You may be able to substitute other tools or equipment for listed items you don't have. Additional common hand tools and clamps may be required to complete the project.

Bill of Materials				
Part	**Finished Size**		**Mat.**	**Qty.**
	T	**W**	**L**	
A side	½"	6⅞"	14⅞"	P	2
B end	½"	6⅞"	7¾"	P	2
C top and bottom	½"	7¾"	15⅞"	P	2
D* long trim	⅛"	1"	8¼"	P	16
E* short trim	⅛"	1"	6¼"	P	16

*Initially cut these parts oversized. Then, trim each to finished size according to the how-to instructions.
Material Key: P—plywood

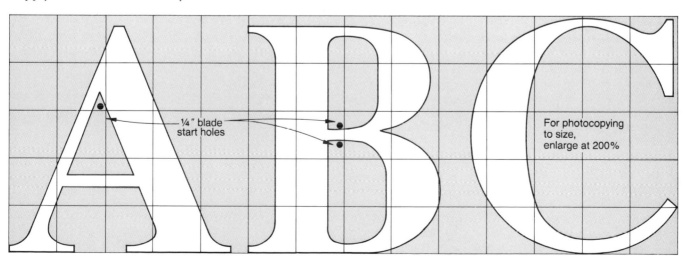

¼" blade start holes

For photocopying to size, enlarge at 200%

BE MINE, VALENTINE

Many of you have told us that the scrollsaw is your first love in woodworking. Here's a heartfelt offering for Valentine's Day combining your first love with a scene of another one.

Note: You'll need ⅛"-thick hardwood or plywood for the heart and silhouette and ¾" hardwood for the base. Also, since the silhouette has some tight corners and small cuts, select a fine, plain-end blade for your scrollsaw. (We used a No. 5 blade, .037×.015", with 14 teeth per inch.)

1. Cut two 4½"-square pieces of ⅛" solid stock or plywood. (We used Baltic birch plywood and solid purpleheart.) Also cut a 3×5" piece of ¾"-thick hardwood for the base. (We selected oak.)

2. Photocopy the full-sized patterns *opposite* for the silhouette, heart, and base. Separate them and affix them to the appropriate stock with spray adhesive or rubber cement. (We applied the silhouette pattern to the plywood and the heart to the purpleheart stock.)

3. Drill ¹⁄₁₆" blade-start holes where indicated on the silhouette pattern. Then, begin scrollsawing with the inside cuts. Complete the silhouette by cutting around the outside line, taking care with small details such as the children's noses or the girl's pigtail. Next, cut out the heart.

4. Drill ¹⁄₁₆" blade-start holes for the two slots in the base where shown on the pattern. Cut out the slots with your scrollsaw, and then saw around the oval outline and sand. For an extra touch, rout a chamfer around the base top.

5. Apply a clear finish to the base, silhouette, and heart. Place the cutouts into the base slots where shown, and then deliver to your sweetheart.

Project Tool List
Tablesaw
Scrollsaw
Portable drill or drill press
  ¹⁄₁₆" bit
Router
  Router table
  Chamfer bit
Finishing sander

Note: We built the project with the tools listed. You may be able to substitute other tools or equipment for listed items you don't have. Additional common hand tools and clamps may be required to complete the project.

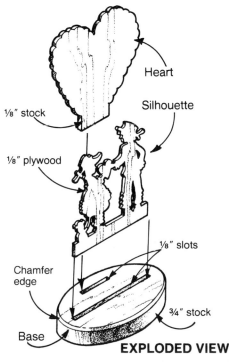

EXPLODED VIEW

FULL-SIZED PATTERNS

Red dots indicate
locations for drilling
1/16" blade start holes

Base

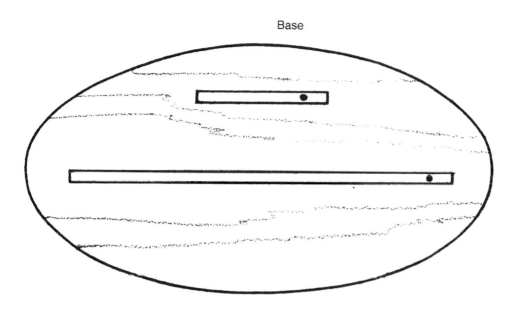

Heart

Silhouette

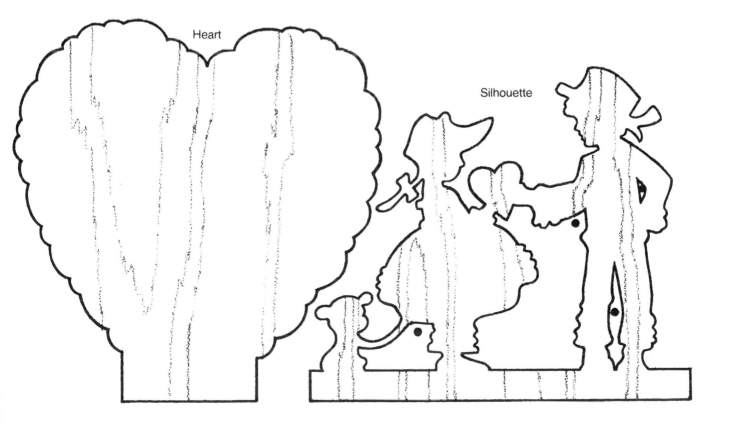

KIDS ON PARADE

Don't let the parade pass you by. Tighten your scrollsaw blade to just the right note, and then pitch in to cut out this energetic marching band in silhouette. Go ahead and whistle while you work— these kids would understand.

Note: You'll need ⅛x5x9½" hardwood stock or plywood (we used Baltic birch plywood) for the cutout and ¾x1½x8¾" hardwood stock for the base. The small inside cuts on this pattern call for a scrollsaw that accepts plain-end blades. (We used a No. 5 blade, .035x.015" with 15 teeth per inch.) If yours doesn't, ask your tool dealer if blade holders are available to adapt your saw to take plain-end blades.

Photocopy the full-sized pattern *opposite*. Attach it to your stock with spray adhesive.

Thin stock lends itself to stack-cutting, so you could cut several bands at once. In fact, you can saw up to five pieces at a time. Hold them together with tape or brads driven into waste areas.

Not only will you have extras for friends, but you'll also find the cutting more controllable. You'll be less likely to cut off the fine details when you work with a thick stack of material.

Drill ⅟₁₆" blade-start holes where indicated on the pattern. Then,

begin cutting out the smallest inside details, such as the spaces between the drum and the drummer or between the youngsters' feet and flowers. Progress to larger details, and cut the outside line last.

To make a base for your silhouette, cut a piece of hardwood (we chose walnut) ¾x1½x8¾". Saw a ⅛" blade kerf ¼" deep along the middle of the topside with a tablesaw. Round the base's top edges with a ¼" round-over bit in a table-mounted router.

Mount the silhouette in the slot and finish. We sprayed on clear lacquer for a natural finish, spraying from several angles to cover all the inside edges.

Project Tool List
Tablesaw
Scrollsaw
Portable drill or drill press
    ¹⁄₁₆" bit
Router
    Router table
¼" round-over bit

Note: *We built the project with the tools listed. You may be able to substitute other tools or equipment for listed items you don't have. Additional common hand tools and clamps may be required to complete the project.*

FULL-SIZED PATTERN

● **Red dots indicate locations to drill ¹⁄₁₆″ blade start holes for interior cuts.**

39

IT'S A GRAND OLD FLAG

Country red, antique white, and deep blue combine for an antique-looking decorator flag you'll be proud to display inside or out. Take a few minutes to scrollsaw it, and then long let it wave.

Note: You'll need 1X10X10" stock (we used pine) and a 10X10" piece of ¼" plywood.

1. Attach a photocopy of the full-sized pattern, *right,* to a 10" length of 1X10 with rubber cement. Place the ends of the stripes at an end of the board.

2. Cut a piece of ¼" plywood to the size of your board. Temporarily attach it to the back of the 1X10 with double-faced tape. Scrollsaw or bandsaw the outside pattern line, and then remove the plywood piece and set it aside.

3. Drill a ⅛" blade-start hole through the board where shown on the pattern. Thread your scrollsaw blade through it (we used a No. 9 blade, .053X.018" with 11.5 teeth per inch), and cut out the star. Then, cut the stripes.

4. Sand the flag, putting a slight round-over on the top-face corners. Apply a coat of barn red to the stripes, but don't paint the edges or the flagpole. Paint the star field

dark blue, and accent the ball atop the flagpole with gold. (We used artist's acrylics.)

5. Paint the top face of the plywood flat white. (We mixed small amounts of brown and yellow with the white to get an aged-looking off-white.) Don't paint the plywood edges.

6. After the paint dries, scuff the flag corners with 150-grit sandpaper for an old, worn look. Brush walnut stain on the flagpole and all edges, including the edges of the plywood piece. Rub thinned walnut stain on the painted areas and quickly wipe it off to create an antique effect.

7. Attach the plywood to the flag with glue or brads. Then, add a wall hanger so you can proudly display Old Glory. If your flag will be going outside, coat it with a weatherproof clear finish.

Project Tool List
Tablesaw
Scrollsaw
Portable drill or drill press
  ⅛" bit

Note: We built the project with the tools listed. You may be able to substitute other tools or equipment for listed items you don't have. Additional common hand tools and clamps may be required to complete the project.

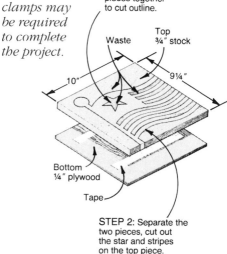

STEP 1: Tape top and bottom pieces together to cut outline.

Waste

Top ¾" stock

10"

9¼"

Bottom ¼" plywood

Tape

STEP 2: Separate the two pieces, cut out the star and stripes on the top piece.

FULL-SIZED PATTERN

Gold

Stain

Blue

White background

⅛" blade-start hole

Red stripes

FLORAL WALL PLAQUES

We think you'll find it fun—and easy—to make these three-dimensional wall hangings. For more details about this nifty scrollsaw technique, refer to the article on *page 18.*

1. Cut two workpiece blanks to 8¼" square from ¾" stock (we used

Honduras mahogany). Cut or rout a ⅛" chamfer along all top outside edges on each.

2. Align the centerpoint, and transfer the full-sized patterns (large photos) on this page and the next to the blanks, using carbon paper.

3. Drill a ¹⁄₁₆" start hole in each blank where shown on the photos.

Using a scrollsaw, cut the disk from within each blank. Then, cut the flower pattern from each disk. Sand a slight round-over on the face of each of the flower pieces and on the inside edge of the outer frame. Now, sand the surfaces smooth.

4. To create the three-dimensional look, first lay the outer frame (good

Sand a slight round-over on edges

Center point

Inset photos *right* and *opposite* show basswood plaques painted with thinned artist's acrylic paint.

Drill a ⅛" hole here

face down) on a flat surface. Lay three ¼"-thick spacers inside the round opening. Position the round disk (good face down) in the circle on the spacers, lining up the grain of the disk with that of the frame. Run a bead of woodworkers' glue around the perimeter of the disk and let dry. (We mixed a small amount of sawdust with the glue to prevent the glue from running between the cracks onto the plaque's face.)

5. Remove the spacers, and place the plaque good face down again.

Now, position each opening from which it was cut. Apply a small bead of glue to the back side of each flower piece and to the disk.

6. Attach a sawtoothed hanger to the back of each plaque. Apply a clear finish of your choice.

Project Tool List
Tablesaw
Scrollsaw
Portable drill or drill press
   ¹⁄₁₆" bit

Router
   Router table
   Chamfer bit
Finishing sander

Note: *We built the project with the tools listed. You may be able to substitute other tools or equipment for listed items you don't have. Additional common hand tools and clamps may be required to complete the project.*

Sand a slight round over on edges

Center point

Drill a ¹⁄₁₆" hole here

WINTER WONDERLAND

In addition to the three R's, youngsters in colder climes study the three S's—sleddin', skatin', and snowman buildin'. These hearty children show their skills on a winter's eve; you can show yours with your scrollsaw.

Note: Re-create our winter. scene with two ¼ x 5½ x 12" pieces of walnut, an 8 x 10" piece of ⅛" Baltic birch plywood, and a 2½ x 7" mirror ⅛" thick. The small inside cuts re-quire plain-end scrollsaw blades.

Attach a photocopy of the full-sized Base pattern, *opposite,* to one piece of walnut with rubber cement or spray adhesive. Tilt your scroll-saw table to 30°.

Drill a ½" hole inside the pond outline, and thread the blade through it. (We used a No. 5 blade, .038 x .016", with 12.5 teeth per inch.) Cut out the inside of the pond, keeping it on the low side of the scrollsaw table. Next, set the saw table to 90°.

Drill ⅟₁₆" blade start holes for the four slots in the upper base part. Cut the slots to match the thickness of your plywood.

Stack the piece you just cut on the other piece of walnut, and trace around the inside of the pond with a pencil. Then, lay out a 2⅜ x 7⅛" rectangle on the bottom layer to encompass the pond outline you just drew. Drill a blade start hole, thread the blade, and cut out the opening.

continued

EXPLODED VIEW

⅛" plywood

30° bevel

⅛" slot

25° bevel

⅛" slot

2½ × 7" mirror

Skater location

¼" stock

25° bevel

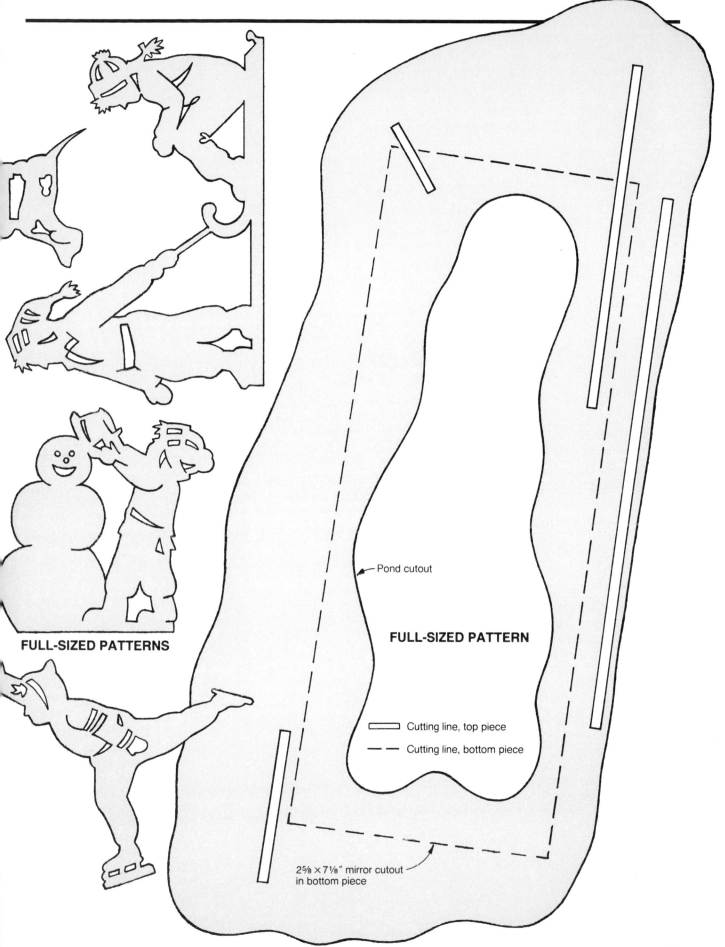

FULL-SIZED PATTERNS

Pond cutout

FULL-SIZED PATTERN

▭ Cutting line, top piece

--- Cutting line, bottom piece

$2\frac{5}{8} \times 7\frac{1}{8}$" mirror cutout in bottom piece

WINTER WONDERLAND
continued

Glue the two walnut pieces together, with the pattern on top. Tilt your scrollsaw table to 25° and then cut around the pattern outline. Keep the patterned piece on the high side of the saw table as you cut.

Transfer the full-sized patterns for the figures and trees (*right* and *page 45*) to your plywood. Drill $\frac{1}{16}$" blade start holes, return the saw table to 90°, and cut, starting with the small inside areas. Test-fit the cutouts in the base slots, and then glue them into place. Apply a clear spray finish such as Deft Wood Finish to the assembled scene and the skater.

From the bottom, fasten the 2½x7" mirror in place with a bead of hotmelt glue. Then, glue the skater into place.

Project Tool List
Tablesaw
Scrollsaw
Portable drill or drill press
 Bits: $\frac{1}{16}$", $\frac{1}{2}$"

Note: *We built the project with the tools listed. You may be able to substitute other tools or equipment for listed items you don't have. Additional common hand tools and clamps may be required to complete the project.*

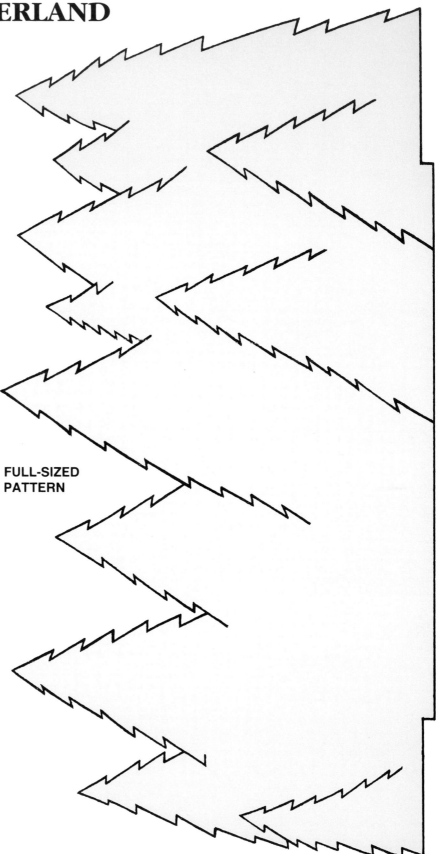

**FULL-SIZED
PATTERN**

LETTER-PERFECT KEY CHAINS

That little plastic key chain from the insurance agent just isn't you, is it? Why not spend a few minutes with your scrollsaw, cutting your initial from laminated hardwoods? Then, make some more for gifts because everyone will want one.

Note: You'll need thin stock to laminate for this project. Plane thicker stock to size, or resaw it.

1. Cut your stock (see the drawing *at right* for thicknesses) and glue up ¼x1½x6" laminations. Photocopy or trace the letter you need from the full-sized alphabet *below.*

2. Adhere the letter to your lamination with spray adhesive. Scrollsaw any interior openings first, drilling start holes as needed. Then, cut around the outline. Sand and apply a clear finish.

3. Remove the bottom ring from a keychain assembly (available from craft suppliers). Open a size 216½ brass screw eye and install it on the chain end. Drill a ⅟₁₆" hole ¼" deep centered in the top edge of the letter. Coat the threads with epoxy, and insert the screw eye.

Project Tool List
Tablesaw
Scrollsaw
Portable drill
 ⅟₁₆" bit

Note: We built the project with the tools listed. You may be able to substitute other tools or equipment for listed items you don't have. Additional common hand tools and clamps may be required to complete the project.

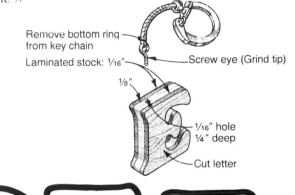

Remove bottom ring from key chain

Laminated stock: ⅟₁₆"

⅛"

Screw eye (Grind tip)

⅟₁₆" hole ¼" deep

Cut letter

FAMILY FEUD SCROLLSAW SILHOUETTE

Before radio and television, home entertainment often amounted to an animated conversation between Mom and Pop in the parlor. What could these two be talking about? Pa's night out? The cost of living? The Cubs' chances? Entertain yourself by cutting this humorous pattern from the past on your scrollsaw. Maybe by the time you're finished, you'll have decided what these two are discussing with such relish.

Note: Cut this authentic old-time pattern from ⅛" Baltic birch plywood. A 5x9" piece will suffice for the stand-up silhouette. You'll also need a ¾x1¼x9" piece of walnut or some other hardwood to make the base.

1. Photocopy the full-sized pattern, *opposite*. Adhere it to your stock with spray adhesive.

2. Since you'll be cutting thin stock, try stack-cutting up to five pieces at a time. You may have more control and be less likely to cut off some of the fine details with the thicker material. Just stack your blanks and tape the edges together with masking tape.

(Some scrollsawers nail their stacks together with small brads outside the pattern area.) Put the pattern on the top piece in the usual fashion.

3. Drill ¹⁄₁₆" blade-start holes where shown on the pattern. Now, begin sawing with the smallest inside cuts, such as Mom's bonnet string, the area between Pop's feet, or the spaces between the chair rockers. We found that a No. 5 blade (.035x.015" with 15 teeth per inch) handled the detailed cutting easily. Complete all inside cuts before sawing the outline.

4. To make a base for your silhouette, cut a piece of hardwood (we chose walnut) ¾x1¼x9". Saw a ⅛" blade kerf ¼" deep along the middle of the topside with a tablesaw. Round the top edges with a ¼" round-over bit in a table-mounted router.

5. Mount the cutout in the slot, and give the project a clear finish. Clear lacquer in a spray can will do the trick. Spray at an angle from top, bottom, and both ends on both sides to cover the edges inside the cutout.

6. Now, put the talkative pair in a conspicuous place. Then, whenever you need some entertainment, you only need to look at them and ask, "What do you suppose they're talking about?"

Project Tool List
Tablesaw
Scrollsaw
Portable drill or drill press
    ¹⁄₁₆" bit
Router
    Router table
    ¼" round-over bit

Note: We built the project with the tools listed. You may be able to substitute other tools or equipment for listed items you don't have. Additional common hand tools and clamps may be required to complete the project.

FULL-SIZED PATTERN

Red dots indicate starting holes for scrollsaw blade.

HEARTS-AND-HARES PICTURE FRAME

You'll cut rabbets and rabbits as you build this delightful frame. Fill it with a photograph or a sampler for a bright accent in any room.

1. Rip a piece of ½"-thick hardwood (we used oak) to 8½" wide, and then crosscut it to 10½" long. From scrap, saw two ½"x½"x14" strips, and *carefully* cut a ¼" rabbet ¼" deep along one edge of each. Miter-cut a 5½" length and a 7½" length from each strip so that the rabbeted edges will meet along the inside.

2. Make two photocopies of the full-sized half-pattern, *below right,* and trim one to the centerline. Match it to the other half, and then tape the two parts together to create a full-sized pattern. Affix it to your workpiece with spray adhesive.

3. Drill the four ⅛" start holes at the corners of the center cutout where indicated on the pattern. Next, drill ⅟₁₆" blade-start holes for the rabbits and heart flowers where shown on the pattern.

4. Cut out the rabbits and flowers with a scroll-saw (we used a No. 5 blade). When you're cutting the flowers, start with the heart-shaped blossom, and then cut down along the stem. Come partway back up the stem and make a figure-8 cut for the leaves.

5. After cutting out the rabbits and flowers, round the frame corners on a disk sander, and then rout all edges indicated on the drawing with a piloted ⅛"

R = ⅜"

Join other side at this line

⅟₁₆" blade-start hole

Cut opening after gluing frame on back side

Centerline

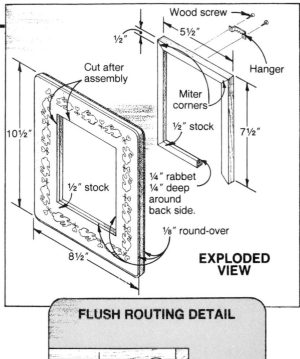

EXPLODED VIEW

- Wood screw
- 5½"
- ½"
- Hanger
- Cut after assembly
- Miter corners
- 10½"
- ½" stock
- ½" stock
- 7½"
- ¼" rabbet ¼" deep around back side.
- 8½"
- ⅛" round-over

round-over bit. Turn the frame facedown, and glue the mitered, rabbeted strips to the backside of the frame as shown on the drawing. (The four ⅛" blade-start holes are locating points.) Cut the opening, using the rabbeted strips as guides.

6. Rout the inside edge of the opening with a flush-trimming bit. The router bit's pilot bearing should ride on the rabbeted strips (see Flush Routing detail, *center right*). Rout a ⅛" round-over along the front inside edge of the opening. Apply a clear finish and attach the hanger.

7. Place a 5x7" piece of single-strength glass, the picture, and a 5x7" piece of cardboard into the back and fasten with glazier points or brads. Cut and attach the leg for a tabletop frame.

Project Tool List
Tablesaw
Scrollsaw
Portable drill or drill press
  Bits: ⅟₁₆", ⅛"
Router
  Router table
  Bits: ⅛" round-over, flush trimming
Disc sander
Finishing sander

Note: *We built the project with the tools listed. You may be able to substitute other tools or equipment for listed items you don't have. Additional common hand tools and clamps may be required to complete the project.*

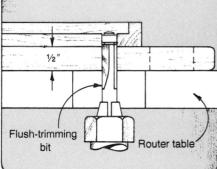

FLUSH ROUTING DETAIL

- ½"
- Flush-trimming bit
- Router table

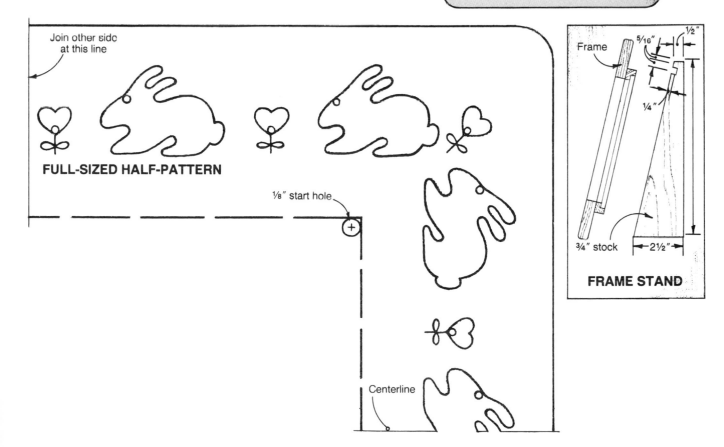

Join other side at this line

FULL-SIZED HALF-PATTERN

⅛" start hole

Centerline

Frame
5/16"
½"
¼"
¾" stock
2½"

FRAME STAND

DOWN BY THE OLD MILL STREAM

Just as these turn-of-the-century youngsters are having fun sailing boats by the water's edge, you'll enjoy scrollsawing their pastime in silhouette. For even more appeal, accent your cutout with painted highlights.

Note: You'll need ⅛"-thick hardwood stock or plywood for the cutout and ¾" hardwood stock for the base. Because of the small inside cuts in this project, you'll need a scrollsaw that will accept plain-end blades to get the job done. (We used a No. 4 blade, .035×.015" with 15 teeth per inch.) Blade holders are available to convert many pin-blade saws to use plain-end blades. Ask your tool dealer.

1. Cut a piece of ⅛" solid stock or plywood (we used Baltic birch; basswood also would be a good choice) to 5½×10". Photocopy the full-sized pattern, *opposite,* and fasten it to the stock with spray adhesive.

2. Drill ¹⁄₁₆" blade-start holes where indicated on the pattern. Then, begin cutting the sailing scene with the smallest inside details, such as the loop in the girl's bonnet string or the inside cuts on the boat she's holding. Progress to larger details, and cut the outside pattern line last.

3. Apply a clear finish. Or, for a different look, paint the scene following the color scheme shown in the photo *above,* or one of your own. Watercolors or thinned artist's acrylic paints applied as washes will give your cutout a faded, aged look. We left the boy's face, hands, and leg, and the girl's hand and legs unpainted on our Baltic birch plywood cutout.

4. For an effective stand, cut a ¾×1¼" piece of hardwood (we chose walnut) to 10" long. Cut a ⅛" groove ¼" deep along the middle of the topside with a tablesaw. If your cutout won't fit the blade kerf, move the fence slightly and make another pass. Round over the top edges with a ¼" round-over bit in a table-mounted router. Finish the stand with a clear oil finish.

Project Tool List
Tablesaw
Scrollsaw
Portable drill or drill press
 ¹⁄₁₆" bit
Router
 Router table
 ¼" round-over bit

Note: We built the project with the tools listed. You may be able to substitute other tools or equipment for listed items you don't have. Additional common hand tools and clamps may be required to complete the project.

FULL-SIZED PATTERN

FOUR NOVEL NAPKIN RINGS

You'll be amazed at how little effort—and even less material—goes into our distinctive napkin rings.

Note: This project requires thin stock. You can resaw or plane thicker stock to the correct thicknesses.

1. Rip and crosscut two ⅜"-thick outside pieces (A) to 2x9". For the ⅛"-thick laminate center (B), purchase or resaw stock of a contrasting color. Rip and crosscut to 2x9". (We used five different kinds of wood for contrasting laminations, but feel free to design your own.) One 9" lamination makes four rings.

2. Glue and clamp the three pieces face-to-face in the arrangement shown on the Laminating and Patterns Layout drawing *opposite*. (We used woodworkers' glue to make up our laminations.)

3. Using carbon paper and the full-sized ring patterns *opposite*, transfer the patterns you want to the top surface of the lamination. Be sure to mark the centerpoint of the inner circle for each ring.

4. Using the marked center-points as guides, bore the center hole of each ring with a 1¼" bit chucked on a drill press. (We used a Forstner bit to ensure a smooth inside cut and minimize sanding. A holesaw would also work if you don't have the correct-size bit.) Back the lamination with a wood scrap as shown in the drawing *opposite, top*. This prevents chip-out on the bottom of the hole. (We also clamped the lamination to the drill-press table.)

5. Cut the rings to shape with a bandsaw or scrollsaw. (We cut

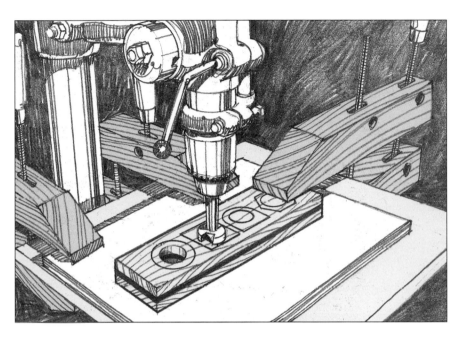

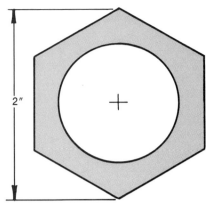

outside the line, and then sanded to the line using a belt sander with 180 grit paper.) If you make just one style of ring and want a perfect match, clamp them together and sand all simultaneously.

6. Sand smooth and round-over the edges, if you wish. (We chucked a 1" drum sander in a drill press to sand the inside of the rings.) Finish as desired. (We strung the rings on a horizontal wire to eliminate handling them, and then applied several thin coats of Deft spray-on lacquer.)

Tablesaw
Scrollsaw or bandsaw
Drill press
   1¼" bit
   1" sanding drum
Belt sander
Finishing sander

Note: *We built the project with the tools listed. You may be able to substitute other tools or equipment for listed items you don't have. Additional common hand tools and clamps may be required to complete the project.*

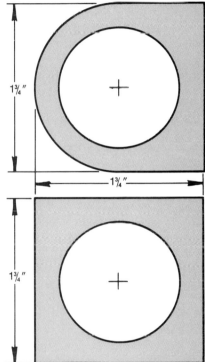

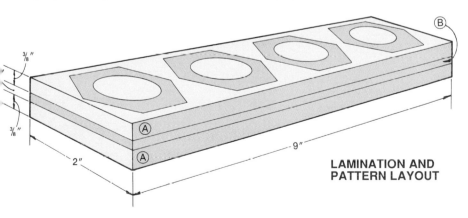

LAMINATION AND PATTERN LAYOUT

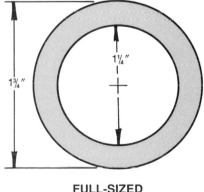

FULL-SIZED PATTERNS

TRAINS, PLANES & AUTOMOBILES

C apture the spirit of America on the move with these stylish silhouettes from the past. They're just right for your den or office.

Nostalgic Locomotive

Let's take a ride on the railroad. The steam locomotive expanded commerce and carried the load for the great westward movement starting late in the 19th century.

Ready your stock

Plane or resaw a 3½ × 30" piece of oak to ¼" thick to make the silhouettes, and a 5¾ × 36" walnut board to ⅜" thick for the plaques. Crosscut 8", 10", and 11" lengths from the oak. Then, cut 10", 11", and 12" lengths from the walnut.

Rout along the edges of the three walnut plaques with a ⁵⁄₃₂" roman ogee bit. Cut a hanging slot in the back of each with a router and keyhole bit. (We cut a centered horizontal slot about 2" long, ¾" from the top edge of the plaque.)

Apply the patterns

Photocopy the full-sized patterns, *above* and on *pages 58–59*, and then attach them to the ¼"-thick oak stock with spray adhesive. Adhere the biplane pattern to the 8" oak piece , the car to the 10" one, and the locomotive to the 11" one. Insure that the pattern is smooth and secure.

continued

AUTOMOBILES
continued

Old-time car

Packard offered motorists power and prestige when this 1926 model rolled off the line. Their motto: "Ask the man who owns one."

Pick a fine blade

The intricate details in these designs call for a narrow blade with about 15 teeth per inch. (We used a No. 4 blade.) If you have a variable- or multiple-speed saw, set a lower speed for easier cutting in the tight-radius curves. Feed the work into the saw more slowly for intricate cutting, too.

Drill 1/16" blade-start holes for the inside cutouts. Start sawing out the smallest inside cuts, and then progress to the larger cutout areas. Finally, cut around the silhouette outline.

FULL-SIZED PATTERN

Early bird

The Wright brothers started it all with a biplane, and two wings were the standard for almost four decades of flight.

Put them on plaques

With the cutting completed, carefully remove the paper patterns and sand the silhouettes as needed.

Be careful when sanding thin sections such as the car's windshield. Sand the walnut plaques.

Center the locomotive cutout on the 12"-long plaque, mark the location, then apply woodworkers' glue sparingly to the back of the silhouette. Clamp it to the plaque with handscrew clamps. Center and attach the automobile to the 11" plaque, and the airplane to the 10" one. When the glue has set, apply a clear oil finish.

Project Tool List

Tablesaw
Scrollsaw
Portable drill or drill press
  $\frac{1}{16}$" bit
Router
  Bits: $\frac{5}{32}$" roman ogee, keyhole
Finishing sander

Note: *We built the project with the tools listed. You may be able to substitute other tools or equipment for listed items you don't have. Additional common hand tools and clamps may be required to complete the project.*

FULL-SIZED PATTERN

NATURE IN THE ROUND

workpiece. Chuck a ³⁄₃₂" bit into your drill, and drill blade-start holes where shown on the pattern.

Thread a scrollsaw blade through one of the holes and begin cutting the openings. (We used a blade with 18 teeth per inch.) When cutting the bird's narrow beak, begin your cut at the head—both at the top and bottom of the beak— and cut toward the end of the beak to avoid breaking it. Continue reinserting the blade in the holes and cutting until all the openings are complete, including the stamen lines in the flower centers.

Finally, form the outside perimeter of the decoration by cutting just outside the marked line, and then sanding to the line. (We used a disk sander.) Remove the paper pattern from the decoration with lacquer thinner. To do this, dampen a cloth with lacquer thinner and press against the paper pattern. Peel off the paper and use the cloth to wipe off any sticky residue on the wood.

To make the stand, follow the three-step cutting process shown *below*. Finish-sand both pieces and apply a finish. (We applied two coats of tung oil.) You might want to hang this project in front of a window.

Capture the beauty of spring with this delightful scrollsaw project. Make the stand to display it or simply hang it in front of a window.

To make your decoration, start with a 6x12" piece of fine-grained hardwood such as cherry or walnut, and plane or resaw it to ³⁄₈" thick. Cut a 6"-square workpiece from this. (Use the remaining 6" square for a second decoration.)

With carbon paper or a photocopy and spray-on adhesive, transfer the full-sized pattern to the

FORMING THE BASE

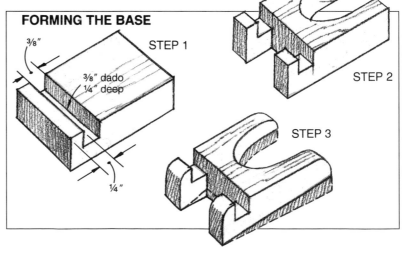

³⁄₈"

³⁄₈" dado
¼" deep

¼"

STEP 1

STEP 2

STEP 3

Drill ³⁄₃₂" holes through the workpiece wherever there is a red dot on the pattern at *left*. This will allow you to insert your scrollsaw blade at these points for cutting each opening to shape.

FULL-SIZED PATTERN

Project Tool List
Tablesaw
    Dado blade or dado set
Scrollsaw
Drill or drill press
    ³⁄₃₂" bit
Belt sander

Note: *We built the project with the tools listed. You may be able to substitute other tools or equipment for listed items you don't have. Additional common hand tools and clamps may be required to complete the project.*

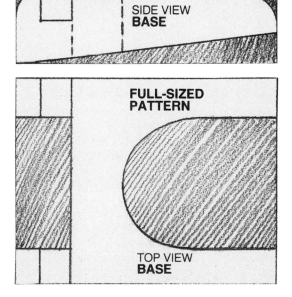

SIDE VIEW
BASE

FULL-SIZED PATTERN

TOP VIEW
BASE

After scrollsawing the pattern, you can easily accomplish touch-up sanding by using an emery nail file or sandpaper wrapped around a stick.

PETAL-POWERED WALL HANGING

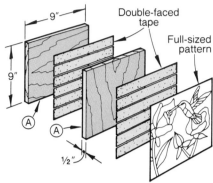

Hang around a blooming garden long enough and you're sure to be mesmerized by the beating of a hummingbird's wings and the darting of its slender body from flower to flower. Now, you can savor that image year-round with our brightly colored wall plaque crafted on the scrollsaw. And, for a depth effect, we've rounded the front edges of the pieces.

Prepare the stock for scrollsawing

1. Cut two pieces of flat ½"-thick pine to 9" square. (To achieve the grain on the flower and bird running in one direction and the grain of the background pieces going in the opposite direction, you'll start with two boards and end up with enough pieces for *two* projects.)

2. Completely cover one face of one of the pieces with double-faced tape (also called carpet tape). With the edges and ends flush, stick the two pieces together, with the grain of one of the pieces

perpendicular to that of the other where shown on the drawing *above.*

3. To enlarge the gridded pattern shown *opposite,* draw a 1" grid measuring 9X9" on a piece of paper. Using the grid pattern as a guide, lay out the shape of the flowers and hummingbird onto the gridded paper. To do this, mark the points where the pattern outline crosses each grid line. Draw lines to connect the points. You'll need three patterns for this project, so either trace two more patterns from the first, or photocopy the first pattern twice.

4. Now, using double-faced tape, adhere one of the full-sized patterns to the face of the top piece.

Scrollsaw and sand the parts to shape

1. To minimize splintering and to prevent small pieces from becoming lodged between the blade and the metal table, add a zero-clearance top to your scrollsaw. (To do this, we cut a piece of ¼" plywood to 13X13". Then, we drilled a ⅛" blade start hole through the middle of the plywood and adhered the plywood to the metal scrollsaw top with double-faced tape.)

2. Scrollsaw the flower and hummingbird patterns to shape. After you cut each piece, separate the two pine sections, remove the

double-faced tape, and mark an X on the *back* side of each. This will come in handy later when sanding the roundovers in the next step.

3. Sand a slight round-over along the *front* edges of each piece— remember, the back side has an X on it. The round-overs add a professional three-dimensional appearance. (To sand the round-overs, we formed a drill clamp out of a scrap 2X4 and 4" carriage bolt, and held it in a woodworker's vise as shown *below.*) You also can hand-sand the round-overs with a palm sander or mount a flexible-sanding disk or drum sander to your drill press.

Sand slight round-overs on the front face of each pattern piece.

Beauty blooms when you paint and adhere the pieces

1. Cut the back (B) to size from ½" plywood. Apply a thin, even coat of woodworkers' glue to the face side of the plywood; then, stick a full-sized pattern to the back (B).

2. Remove the double-faced tape and/or the pattern from the front of the sanded pieces. In a well-ventilated area, dampen a cloth with lacquer thinner, and clean each piece (the double-faced tape tends to leave a sticky residue).

3. Group all the green pieces together and paint them. (We used fast-dry enamel spray paint. To allow the grain to show through slightly, we sprayed on the first coat of paint and immediately wiped off most of it with a clean cloth. Later, we applied a light second coat without wiping it off.) Repeat for the red, brown, and white pieces.

4. Use woodworker's glue to adhere the pieces, one at a time, to the paper pattern glued to the ½" plywood as shown *right*.

5. After gluing all the pieces in place, check for 90° corners. Trim as necessary.

Add the frame, and apply the finish

1. Cut two pieces of ½" pine to 1¼" wide by 22" long for the frame pieces (C). Rout ¼" round-overs along one edge of each.

2. Miter-cut the four frame pieces to length. Glue and clamp the frame pieces to the center portion.

3. To allow for hanging the project, drill a ¼" hole ½" deep at an upward angle on the back side of the frame where shown in the Hole detail accompanying the Exploded View drawing.

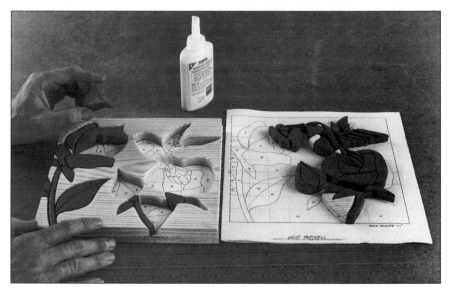

Apply glue to the pattern pieces and adhere them to the backing board.

4. To avoid runs, spray on several light coats of a clear finish (we used Deft, an aerosol lacquer).

Project Tool List
Tablesaw
Scrollsaw
Portable drill or drill press
  Bits: ⅛", ¼"
  Sanding disc
Router

Router table
¼" round-over bit
Finishing sander

Note: *We built the project with the tools listed. You may be able to substitute other tools or equipment for listed items you don't have. Additional common hand tools and clamps may be required to complete the project.*

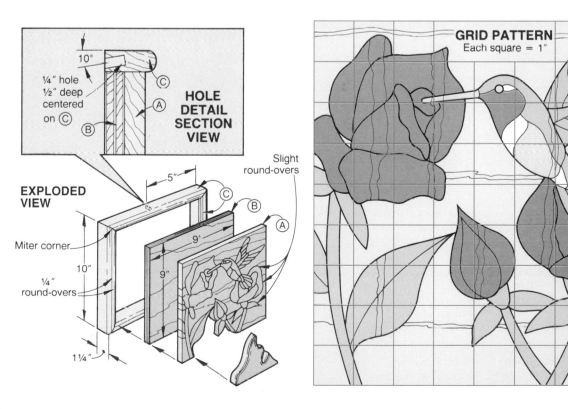

DOLLAR-SAVING MONEY CLIPS

Cash in on your wood-
working talents with a fun
project you can complete in an
afternoon. Using scrap woods
and our source for money clips,
you can easily personalize an
entire year's worth of gifts in no
time at all.

*Note: You can buy fully
assembled money clips. See the
Buying Guide for our mail-order
source.*

**Find a mother lode of resources
in your scrap bin**

1. Make working copies of the
six designs. (We photocopied
ours.) Next, determine the number
and colors of woods needed for
each inlay. The trout, flying eagle,
and dog require a dark and light
wood. The flying ducks, oak
branch, and bald eagle require four
contrasting woods. (For the dog
and flying eagle inlays pictured
above, we used walnut and oak.

We chose oak, maple, walnut, and
cherry for the ducks.)

2. For safety, start with ¾"-thick
scrap pieces measuring at least 12"
long. Rip them 1¹⁄₁₆" wide, and then
resaw ³⁄₁₆"-thick strips from these
pieces. Next, sand the strips to a
uniform ⅛" thickness. (We laid our
strips on a flat surface and sanded
them simultaneously, using 150-,
180-, and 220-grit sandpaper.) Now,
crosscut the strips into 2¹⁄₁₆"-long
blanks.

Saw into all stopped lines

FLYING EAGLE

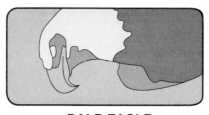

BALD EAGLE

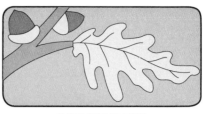

OAK BRANCH

3. Stack the wood blanks together face-to-face. (We used thin double-faced cellophane tape between the blanks, but you may temporarily adhere them with rubber cement or spray adhesive.) Now, sand the edges of each blank stack to match the size of the money clips.

4. Make an auxiliary top for your scrollsaw table. (We made ours from ⅛"-thick hardboard.) Drill a ¹⁄₁₆" hole through this top for the blade, and then tape it to your saw's table.

5. Apply a mist coat of spray adhesive to the pattern's back. Center, and then adhere it to the top blank of each stack. Drill a blade start hole through the pattern and blank stack. (We drilled through areas where a hole was least visible.)

6. Thread your scrollsaw blade through the start hole, and then attach it to the saw. (We used a No. 2/0 blade with 20 to 23 teeth per inch.) If you have a variable-speed saw, set it at a medium or slow speed. To bevel-cut the stacked pieces (which will give you a better-looking finished inlay), tilt your scrollsaw table 6½° to the left. Cut out the inlay in a counter-clockwise direction. (We sawed around the smaller pieces, cut into the stopped lines as we worked, and then cut out the bigger pieces last.) Be careful not to lose the small pieces.

Mix and match parts for color and contrast

1. Carefully separate the stack so as not to break the fragile parts. If you have trouble pulling apart some of the small pieces, dip them in lacquer thinner to dissolve the adhesive.

2. Arrange the cutout parts on waxed paper. Make up the inlay combinations by interchanging parts from the different wood layers. To assemble two-part inlays such as the dog, you place the dark-colored dog inside the light background and vice versa. When designs have three or more wood species, assemble several versions and select the combinations that appeal most to you. For example, of the four flying ducks combinations, we preferred the inlay with the lightest (maple) sun and darkest (walnut) ducks.

3. Wrap a strip of ⅛"-wide masking tape around the outside edge of each assembled inlay to hold it together. Next, mix a small amount of five-minute epoxy and place it on top of each inlay. Now, carefully work the epoxy down into the saw kerfs between the inlay parts.

4. After the epoxy cures, remove the masking tape, and sand both sides of the inlay flat. Now, finish-sand the top face and round over the top edges with 220- and 320-grit sandpaper on a pad sander.

5. Apply the finish of your choice. (We brushed on one coat of sanding sealer and two coats of

semigloss polyurethane. We sanded with 320-grit sandpaper after each coat dried.) If you wish to use an oil finish, apply it *after* you epoxy the inlay to the money-clip face.

6. To adhere the inlay to the money clip, first clean the flat metal surface with lacquer thinner. Next, lightly sand the clip face with 220-grit sandpaper, being careful not to touch it with your fingers.

7. Apply a thin, uniform layer of epoxy to the clip face and the underside of the inlay. Join the two parts and press together. Hold or tape the inlay firmly to the clip until the epoxy sets. Immediately remove any epoxy squeeze-out.

Buying Guide:
• **Money clips.** Assembled clips with folding knife and nail file. Catalog No. 1226. For current prices, contact Meisel Hardware Specialties, P.O. Box 70-WEW, Mound, MN 55364-0070.

Project Tool List
Tablesaw
Scrollsaw
Portable drill or drill press
   ¹⁄₁₆" bit
Finishing sander

***Note:** We built the project with the tools listed. You may be able to substitute other tools or equipment for listed items you don't have. Additional common hand tools and clamps may be required to complete the project.*

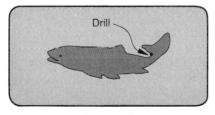

TROUT

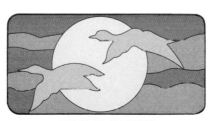

FLYING DUCKS

DOG

MAN-IN-THE-MOON CLOCK

Hollywood has turned out some star-studded creations over the years. Here's one you can produce yourself. Our whimsical man-in-the-moon clock looks just right in a child's room; grown-ups who appreciate flights of fancy will love it, too.

Note: We made our clock from basswood. Pine would work, too, since it will be painted. You'll need a piece ¾×7×8" for the clock body, one that's ⅜×5×7" for the moon and star overlays, and a 1½×1½×6" piece for the base. (We planed thicker stock for the ⅜" material, and laminated two ¾"-thick pieces together for the 1½" base.) A No. 7 scrollsaw blade, .043×.016" with 12 teeth per inch, will handle the cutting.

Photocopy the full-sized pattern *opposite*. Now, trace the outside oval shape of the body, the clock-hole centerpoint, and the circled numbers inside the stars onto the ¾" board. Next, trace the moon and the stars (including the circled numbers) onto the ⅜" material, and the base outline onto your 1½" stock.

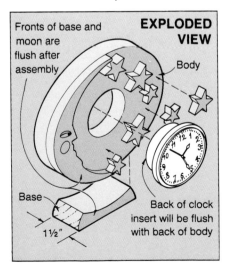

Fronts of base and moon are flush after assembly

EXPLODED VIEW

Body

Base

1½"

Back of clock insert will be flush with back of body

Saw around the body outline, and cut out the base. Then, cut out the moon and star shapes. Notice that star number 1 connects to the moon—cut them as one piece.

Bore the 2⅜"-diameter hole for the clock insert with a Forstner bit or holesaw chucked into a drill press. Whichever you use, be sure to back the workpiece with scrap-wood, and clamp it firmly to the drill-press table.

Position the moon on the body, attaching it temporarily with double-faced tape. Sand the edges flush, and then sand the body and base so they fit together tightly. Glue the base to the body. Set the front of the base flush with the front of the moon, and then remove the moon from the body.

Sand all surfaces. Then, redraw the circled numbers on the body, and number the stars on their backs to help position them.

Paint the body and base black (we used artist's acrylics). Don't paint the circled numbers and the area where the moon will be glued on. Paint the front and edges of the moon off-white. Add the cheek and eye details after the paint dries. As you paint the fronts and edges of the stars white, don't forget to paint the portions on the backs of stars 2, 4, and 8 that extend past the edge of the body. When dry, glue the moon and stars into place.

Later, spray on a semigloss clear finish to protect the paint and add a bit of luster. After the finish dries, install the clock insert.

Buying Guide
• **Clock insert.** Ready-to-install unit with quartz movement, black case and bezel, and black face with white hands and numerals; runs on one type N battery (included). Order Item No. 71165. For current prices, contact U.S. Klockit, P.O. Box 636, Lake Geneva, WI 53147, or call 800-556-2548.

Project Tool List
Tablesaw
Scrollsaw
Drill press
   2⅜" bit
Belt sander
Finishing sander

Note: *We built the project using the tools listed. You may be able to substitute other tools or equipment for listed items you don't have. Additional common hand tools and clamps may be required to complete the project.*

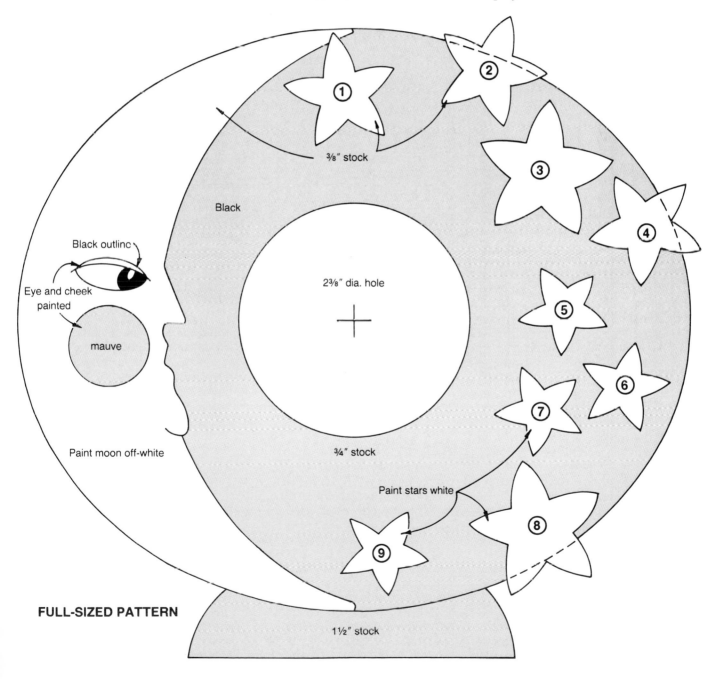

Black outline

Eye and cheek painted

mauve

Black

③⁄₈" stock

2⅜" dia. hole

Paint moon off-white

¾" stock

Paint stars white

FULL-SIZED PATTERN

1½" stock

OLD-WORLD WINDMILL

Here's a scrollsawed plaque with something different—depth. Cutouts mounted on three levels make this windmill scene an eyecatcher. You'll breeze through the cutting, too, because you won't have to stop to thread the blade through tiny holes. You'll complete this project *without* any inside cuts, not even for the window openings.

You'll need a ⅛×8×10" piece of Baltic birch plywood (available at hobby shops) and a 12" piece of 1×12 rough-sawed cedar. Designers Roy King and Scott Kochendorfer recommend cutting the pattern with a No. 2/0 scrollsaw blade (.022×.010" with 28 teeth per inch). For smoothest sawing overlay your saw's table with a piece of smooth plywood with a zero-clearance blade hole.

Photocopy the full-sized patterns, *opposite*, and adhere them to the plywood with spray adhesive. Cut out the parts.

When cutting the windmill building (A), start at the upper left window where shown. Cut the four window panes, leaving the muntins attached at the right side of the window.

Back out of the window entry cut, and saw down the left side until you reach the next window entry. Cut as before, back out, and continue around the building, cutting the door and the other window as you come to them.

After you've cut out the entire piece, saw the horizontal lines. Saw in along each line, and then carefully back out.

Cut the open areas on the windmill support (B) by entering on the lines shown along the top. Scrollsaw the windmill sails (C), cutting each long detail line as you come to it. Then, go back and cut the short detail lines.

Change to a heavier scrollsaw blade. Tilt the saw table to 30°, and saw a freeform edge on the 1×12 plaque, maintaining an 8½×8½" area

in the center. With the rough side up, keep the plaque on the high side of the table as you saw. Install a wall hanger on back of the plaque.

Now, assemble the scene

After removing the patterns, glue the windmill building (A) and large cloud (G) where indicated on the Plaque Layout drawing. Add the path sides (D and E) and the spacer (K). Next, glue the single tree (I) and double tree (J) to the back of the ground line (H), aligning them as indicated.

Glue the ground line and trees into position, and then glue the windmill support (B) to the building. Glue spacer (L) to the back of the small cloud (F), and glue these pieces to the plaque.

Complete the assembly by gluing the sails to the spacer (K). Spray on

a clear finish from several angles, covering all edges.

Buying guide

• **More patterns.** Scroller offers many patterns in various difficulty ratings. For a catalog, send $2.00 for postage and handling to Scroller Catalog, 9033 S. Nashville, Oak Lawn, IL 60453. No phone orders, please.

Project Tool List
Tablesaw
Scrollsaw

Note: We built the project using the tools listed. You may be able to substitute other tools or equipment for listed items you don't have. Additional common hand tools and clamps may be required to complete the project.

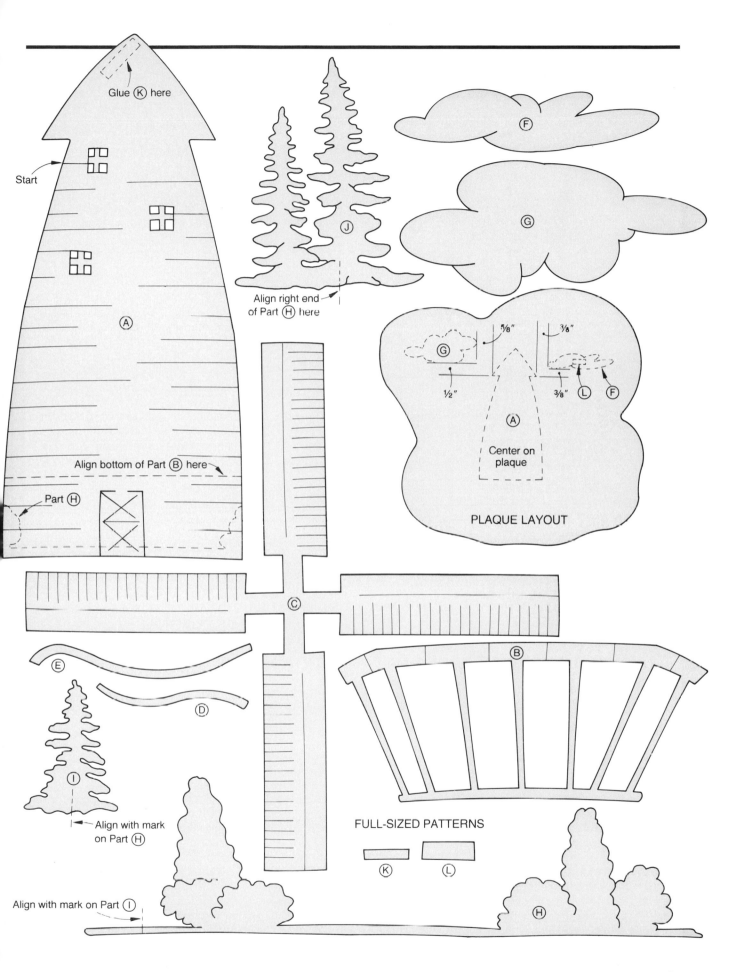

Glue (K) here

Start

Align right end
of Part (H) here

(F)

(G)

(A)

(J)

5/8"   3/8"

(G)

1/2"   3/8"   (L)   (F)

(A)

Center on
plaque

PLAQUE LAYOUT

Align bottom of Part (B) here

Part (H)

(C)

(E)

(D)

(B)

(I)

Align with mark
on Part (H)

FULL-SIZED PATTERNS

(K)   (L)

Align with mark on Part (I)

(H)

TABLETOP TOM

the tail fan on the ¼" stock, trace around the half-pattern, flop the pattern over, align, and trace the other half of the pattern onto the plywood. See the Exploded View drawing for the shape of the finished tail fan.

3. Cut the tail fan and body pieces to shape (we used a scrollsaw and a No. 7 blade—.043×.016"—with 12 teeth per inch). You also could use a bandsaw equipped with a ⅛" blade for the outline and a coping saw for the hole in front of the neck. (We found it easiest to cut the arcs of the two pieces to shape, and then cut each V-shaped indentation.)

When cutting the notches in the two parts, *remember that the notch width needs to be the same as the thickness of the stock you're using.* (Since we used ¼" material for our project, we show ¼" notches on our full-sized patterns; adjust if necessary.)

4. Fill any voids along the edges with wood putty. Sand the faces and edges of both pieces with 150- and then 220-grit sandpaper. Apply a clear finish.

Buying Guide
• **Void-free ¼" birch plywood.** ¼×9×9", Stock No. W1192T, two pieces (enough for one turkey). For current prices, contact Heritage Building Specialties, 205 North Cascade, Fergus Falls, MN 56537, or call 800-524-4184.

Project Tool List
Scrollsaw or bandsaw
Finishing sander
Portable drill
  ⅛" bit

Note: *We built the project with the tools listed. You may be able to substitute other tools or equipment for listed items you don't have. Additional common hand tools and clamps may be required to complete the project.*

Add a festive decoration to this year's Thanksgiving table with our super simple two-part cutout. Using your scrollsaw or bandsaw, you're just minutes away from a completed project, leaving you plenty of time to carve the real turkey (and maybe do a little nibbling just to make sure it's done).

1. Using carbon paper, transfer paper, or two photocopies of the pattern and spray adhesive (we used 3M Super 77 spray adhesive), transfer the two turkey patterns (the entire body and the tail fan) to posterboard. Cut the patterns to shape to form the two templates. (Since we planned on making several turkeys, we made poster-board templates; for just one turkey, transfer the two patterns directly to your wood.)

2. Use the templates to transfer the patterns to ¼" stock. (See the Buying Guide for our source of void-free birch plywood.) To form

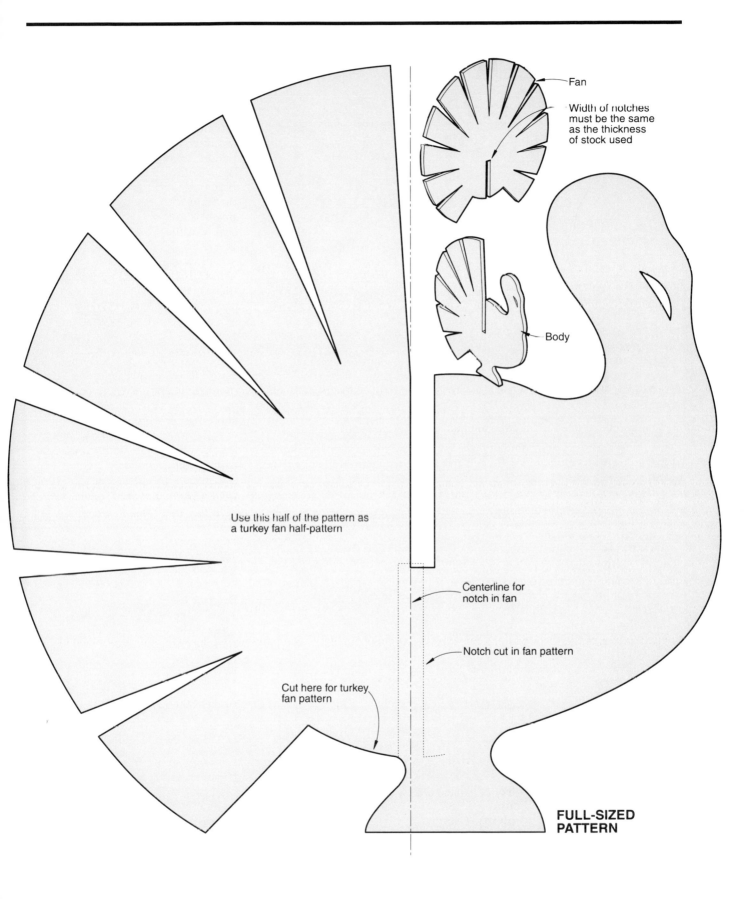

Fan

Width of notches must be the same as the thickness of stock used

Body

Use this half of the pattern as a turkey fan half-pattern

Centerline for notch in fan

Notch cut in fan pattern

Cut here for turkey fan pattern

FULL-SIZED PATTERN

THREE-DIMENSION INVENTION

Usher in the holiday season with three interlocking ornaments you can scrollsaw in your shop. Then, call on an old friend—Rit dye—to introduce a little color to your projects.

Put your scrollsaw to work on thin plywood

1. Copy the patterns *opposite.* (We photocopied ours.) Cut out the patterns, leaving a ¼" margin around the outside. Make two copies of the star pattern and join along the centerline.

2. Saw 4" squares from ⅛"-thick Baltic birch plywood for the heart and star; 4½" squares for the snowflake. If you enlarge the patterns, cut correspondingly larger squares. (We stack-cut six of each ornament at one time.)

3. Apply a light coat of adhesive to the back of each pattern copy, and then adhere each one to the face of a square. Make stacks of squares of each size and place a patterned square on top of each stack. Drive ¾"×17 brads or 4d finish nails through the waste areas to hold the stacks together. To avoid tear out, adhere a backup square or scrap piece to the bottom of each stack. (We used hotmelt glue.)

4. Using your drill press, drill the start holes, string holes, and decorative holes through the stacks where instructed on the patterns.

5. To cut out the star, thread your scrollsaw blade through Start Hole 1, and saw along the inside line to remove the waste. (We used a No. 5R reverse-tooth blade with 12½" teeth per inch.) Cut into and back out of the stop cuts in each point as you saw around the inside.

Next, insert the blade through Start Hole 2, and cut between the two stars. Saw around the outside of the star. Cut the slits leading from the ³⁄₆₄"-string holes to the star edge.

6. Follow the same procedures to cut out the heart and snowflake.

Note the additional entry hole on the three-part snowflake.

Have fun dyeing, tying

1. Separate the plywood layers. Remove the paper patterns, and lightly sand all pieces.

2. Select and mix your dyes for each ornament. (We mixed 1 cup of liquid Rit dye to two cups of hot

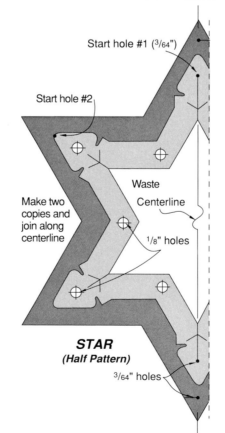

Start hole #1 (³⁄₆₄")

Start hole #2

Make two copies and join along centerline

Waste

Centerline

⅛" holes

STAR
(Half Pattern)

³⁄₆₄" holes

Loop thread through holes

Right end

Left end

Tie loose ends into knot

water.) Pour the dye mixtures into flat-bottom pans. Tie a thread to each piece, place them in the dye baths, and let set for 10 minutes or until the parts reach the desired color. You may want to experiment with plywood scraps first. Turn the parts frequently to ensure uniform coloring. Finally, remove the parts, rinse with water, and hang up to dry. (At the same time, we dyed lengths of white thread to match the ornaments' colors, and used them for stringing.)

3. Cut two 4" lengths of thread for each ornament. To string, reassemble the ornament. Next, pull about half of one thread through the small string hole at one end, and then follow the illustrations *opposite.* Pull thread ends snug, tie a square knot, and cut off the excess, leaving ¼"-long tails. Repeat the steps on the opposite end. String a longer thread through one end and use it for hanging the ornament.

4. To display the ornaments, turn the inner pieces of the two-part ornaments 90° to the outer piece, and press the points into place to make them stay. To display the snowflake, turn the three parts about 60° from each other.

Supplies:
Stock: ⅛"-thick Baltic birch plywood; Materials: dyes, thread.

Project Tool List
Tablesaw
Scrollsaw
Drill press
  Bits: ¾₄", ³⁄₃₂", ⅛"

Note: *We built the project using the tools listed. You may be able to substitute other tools or equipment for listed items you don't have. Additional common hand tools and clamps may be required to complete the project.*

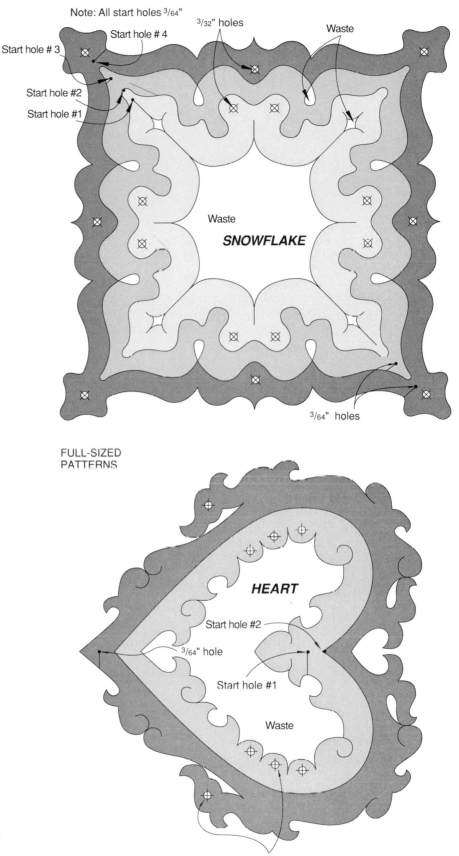

Note: All start holes ³⁄₆₄"

Start hole # 4   ³⁄₃₂" holes   Waste

Start hole # 3

Start hole #2

Start hole #1

Waste

SNOWFLAKE

³⁄₆₄" holes

FULL-SIZED PATTERNS

HEART

Start hole #2

³⁄₆₄" hole

Start hole #1

Waste

DECORATIVE SCROLLSAW PROJECTS

Scrollsawing enables you to create unusual and delightful decorative pieces. Here you'll find a sampling of great projects sure to please family and friends alike.

SOUTHWEST LANDSCAPE

When she's not hiking or fishing in the mountains in her home state of New Mexico, Andrea Miller is busy in her woodshop, building projects to market at craft fairs in Santa Fe and Albuquerque. We were pleased when Andrea decided to share one of her biggest sellers, "Desert Magic," with us. Here's hoping you'll enjoy displaying this decorative accessory in your home.

Note: You'll need ½" stock for this project. You can plane or resaw thicker stock to size.

Make some mountains for yourself

1. Cut five pieces of heavy paper to 8x14", and draw a 1" grid on each. Using the grid pattern on *page 76* for reference, lay out one landscape section on each piece of paper. To do this, mark the points where the pattern outline crosses each grid line. Draw lines to connect the points. Cut the patterns to shape. Repeat the process with a 3x10" piece of paper to form the template for the base pieces.

2. Position the paper templates on the species of hardwood noted on the grid drawing, and trace the outline of each landscape section onto the stock. (We took a close look at our stock before tracing and chose the portion of the board with the most striking grain pattern.)

3. Bandsaw the five landscape sections (A through E) and the five base pieces (F) to shape. (We used a ⅛"-wide blade to cut the heavily contoured top edge of each landscape section to shape. Then, we switched to a ⅜"-wide blade to cut the curves along the bottom edge of each landscape section and to cut the base pieces to shape. The ⅜" blade ensures a smoother cut and less sanding later when fitting together the pieces.)

4. Transfer the full-sized cactus pattern to ⅛" walnut stock, and cut the cactus to shape.

Assemble and apply finish before sunset

1. Finish-sand each piece. Glue and clamp together the five base pieces with the edges and ends flush. Glue and clamp together the landscape sections where shown on the gridded drawing. Wipe off squeeze-out with a damp cloth. (When gluing together the land-scape sections, keep the glue about ½" away from the contoured top edge to eliminate hard-to-get-at squeeze-out.)

2. After the glue dries, check the fit of the bottom of the landscape scene against the top portion of the base. Sand the mating surfaces for a snug fit. (We used a drum sander to sand the top edge of the base, and a belt sander to sand the bottom edge of the scene. Sand until you have a gap-free fit.

3. Glue the scene to the base, wiping off excess glue with a damp cloth. Glue the cactus to the scene.

4. Finish-sand the assembly. Finally, apply the finish.

Project Tool List
Scrollsaw or bandsaw
Drill press
Sanding drum
Belt sander
Finishing sander

Note: We built the project with the tools listed. You may be able to substitute other tools or equipment for listed items you don't have. Additional common hand tools and clamps may be required to complete the project.

continued

SOUTHWEST LANDSCAPE
continued

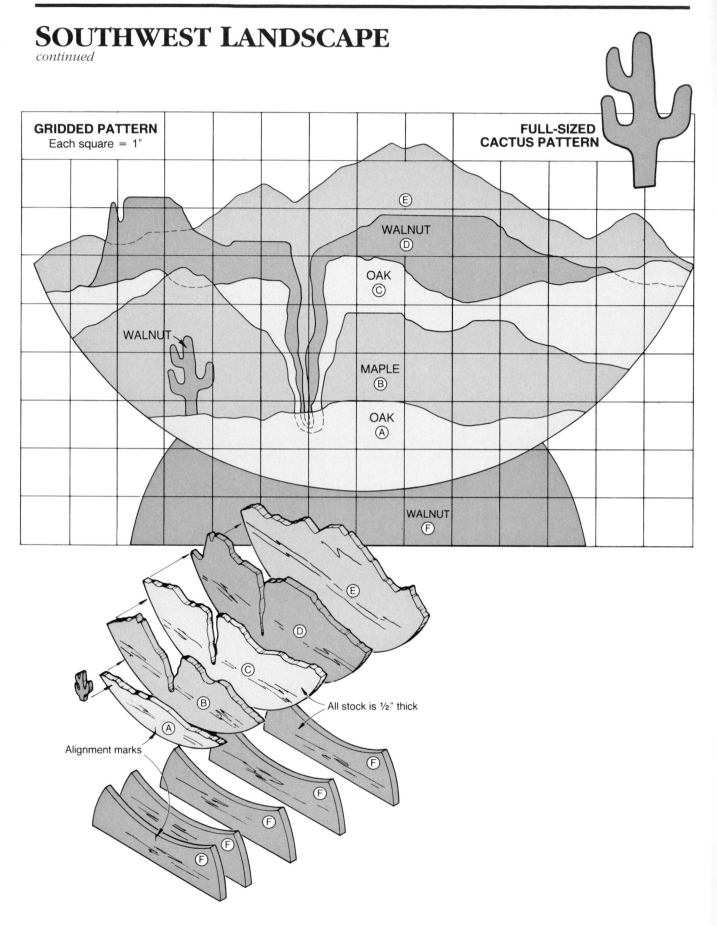

GRIDDED PATTERN
Each square = 1"

**FULL-SIZED
CACTUS PATTERN**

E

WALNUT
D

OAK
C

WALNUT

MAPLE
B

OAK
A

WALNUT
F

E

D

C

B

A

All stock is ½" thick

Alignment marks

F

F

F

F

F

PENGUINS ON PARADE

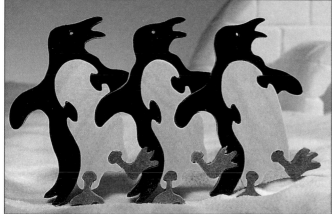

Brighten your day with a trio of laughable, easy-to-scrollsaw characters

1. Copy the pattern *below.* (We set our enlarging photocopier for a 150-percent enlargement. That made our penguins 5" tall and 10" wide.)

2. Rip and crosscut a piece of ½"-thick Baltic birch plywood to a size slightly larger than your pattern. Using spray adhesive or rubber cement, adhere the pattern to the plywood.

3. Scrollsaw around the outside of the pattern and remove the waste. (We used a No. 5R [reverse tooth] blade.) Next, saw out the individual penguin parts. Drill the ¹⁄₁₆" eye holes. Remove the pattern from the pieces.

4. Finish-sand all surfaces and edges. (We used a ½"-diameter sanding drum to smooth the curved surfaces. Do not oversand the interlocking parts—you don't want them fitting too loose.) Next, seal all surfaces of the plywood with a coat of sanding sealer or polyurethane.

5. Paint your penguins. (We left the bellies natural but sprayed the bodies black and feet orange.) Thoroughly cover all sides and edges on each body part. After the paint dries, reassemble the interlocking parts. Stand your laughable trio upright to parade.

Supplies
Stock: ½" Baltic birch plywood; Materials: polyurethane, paint.

Project Tool List
Tablesaw
Scrollsaw
Portable drill
   ¹⁄₁₆" bit
   ½" sanding drum

Note: *We built the project using the tools listed. You may be able to substitute other tools or equipment for listed items you don't have. Additional common hand tools and clamps may be required to complete the project.*

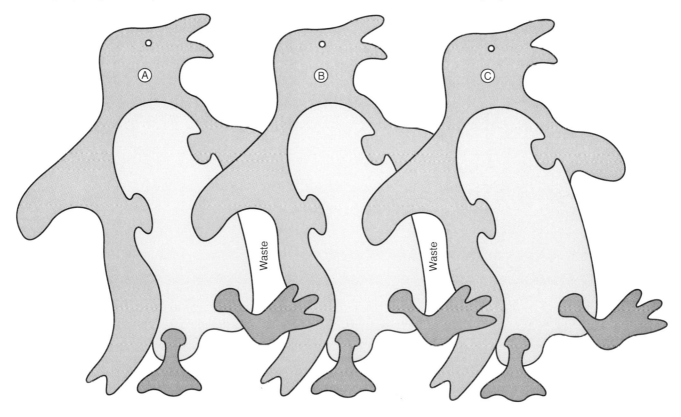

PAINT IT AGAIN (AND AGAIN), SAM

From scrollsaw to spray varnish, our Uncle Sam stands finished in only two hours. Large or small, he's an all-American winner for birthday-party favors or a Fourth of July picnic-table decoration.

Palette

Delta Ceramcoat Colors
    Black
BR   Burgundy Rose 2123
LI   Light Ivory 2401
MF   Medium Flesh 2126
MD   Midnight 2114
Delta Metallics
NG   Nugget Gold

Brushes

¼" synthetic flat
No. 10/0 synthetic liner
No. 2 fabric
No. 2 stencil

Supplies

1x6x12" pine
¼x5½" dowel
⅜x7½" dowel
Medium-tipped permanent
    black marking pen
Small paper flag
Scrap of red raffia for bow
10" of gold star garland
6x8" piece of canvas
Hotmelt adhesive
Matte-finish spray varnish

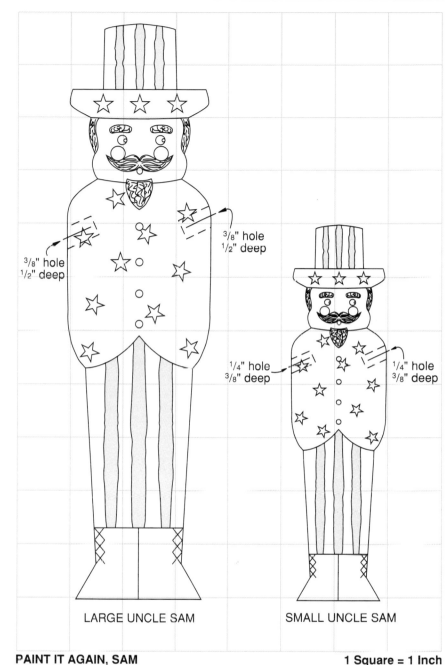

LARGE UNCLE SAM   SMALL UNCLE SAM

PAINT IT AGAIN, SAM   1 Square = 1 Inch

Start with raw wood

After duplicating the Uncle Sam patterns with tracing paper, copy the outlines with transfer paper onto a 12"-long piece of 1x6 pine (actual size: ¾x5½"). Cut out the pieces with a scrollsaw, using a No. 5 blade. Then, cut two 2½"-long pieces of ¼" dowel for the small Sam's arms, and two 3½"-long pieces of ⅜" dowel for the larger Sam's arms. Drill ¼" and ⅜" holes where shown on the patterns. Sand all surfaces with the grain, using 100- and then 150-grit sandpaper. Remove dust with a tack cloth. Then, copy pattern details onto the cutouts, using transfer paper.

Have fun painting

Thin your paints with water 5:1. Using a ¼"-wide flat brush, paint the cutout backs MD.

Clothes: *Paint the details on the front and the edges of the cutouts.* With a ¼" flat brush base-coat the jacket and hat brim MD, the hat top and slacks LI, and the boots Black. With a No. 10/0 liner brush and LI, add boot laces, and paint a line to separate the boots. (Project designer Peggy Kahler says kids prefer a white chalk pencil when making boot laces.)

After dipping a No. 2 fabric brush into BR, pounce the brush up and down on a paper towel to remove excess paint. Using the same pouncing motion, make stripes on Uncle Sam's hat and slacks. Dip the handle end of a brush in BR, and dot the buttons on his jacket. Allow the paints to dry thoroughly.

To simplify painting the stars on the hat brim and jacket, Peggy cuts star stencils. Stencil LI stars with a No. 2 stencil brush.

continued

79

PAINT IT AGAIN (AND AGAIN), SAM
continued

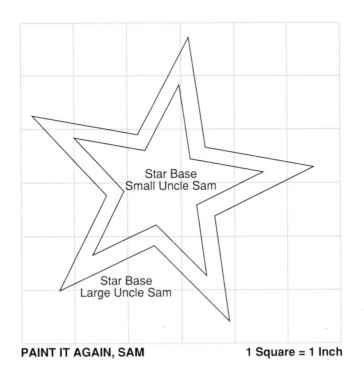

Star Base
Small Uncle Sam

Star Base
Large Uncle Sam

PAINT IT AGAIN, SAM　　　　　　　　**1 Square = 1 Inch**

Face and arms: Using a ¼" flat brush, base-coat Uncle Sam's face MF and the sleeve portion of the arm dowels MD. For hands, apply MF on the bottom ⅜" of the small Sam's arms and the bottom ½" of the larger Sam's arms. (Peggy tapes off the sleeve area with transparent tape to get a straight line around the wrist.) Base-coat the hair, eyebrows, mustache, and goatee LI. (Or, cut a stencil for the mustache and goatee.) Then, add detail lines with a black permanent marking pen.

Next, using the handle end of a brush, dot the eyes Black and the mouth BR. Dip a stylus into LI, and dot a small highlight in each eye at the 3 o'clock position. Lightly blush cheeks BR, using a fabric brush. Wipe off most of the paint from the fabric brush before brushing on the cheek color.

Finish with pride

To remove fuzz raised by the acrylic paints, lightly sand with a paper grocery sack. Remove the dust with a tack cloth. Glue arms into the body. Then, spray Uncle Sam with two coats of matte-finish varnish.

Cut the star base from canvas (or pine, if you prefer), and paint the base NG. Using hotmelt adhesive, glue the base to Uncle Sam's boots. Tie a red raffia bow around a small flag, and glue the flagpole to Sam's left hand. (Check party-favor or paper-goods shops for paper flags and star garland.) Next, glue one 2½" length of star garland to the smaller Sam's right hand, and three 2½" lengths of star garland to the larger Sam's right hand.

Project Tool List
Scrollsaw
Portable drill or drill press
　Bits: ¼", ⅜"
Finishing sander

Note: *We built the project with the tools listed. You may be able to substitute other tools or equipment for listed items you don't have. Additional common hand tools and clamps may be required to complete the project.*

PEGASAURUS PUZZLE

No need to fear our dinosaur. Designed with toddlers in mind, this prehistoric playmate provides hours of safe entertainment.

continued

PEGASAURUS PUZZLE
continued

PALETTE	Brushes	¼×8⅜×14¼" hardboard
Delta Ceramcoat Colors	½" synthetic flat	⅜×17" dowel
Black	No. 4 synthetic round	#18×¾" brads
OR Orange 2026	**Supplies**	Water-based fruitwood stain
TU Turquoise 2012	1×4×15" pine,	Matte-finish spray varnish
White	1×8×13" pine	Felt

Start with raw wood

Begin by building a puzzle frame from ½"-wide strips ripped from 1×4 pine. Sand with the grain using 120-grit sandpaper. Cut two 14¼"-long pieces and two 8⅜"-long pieces—each with 45° mitered ends. Then, cut ¼"-thick hardboard to 8⅜×14¼". Glue the pieces together and nail through the hardboard. (Project designer Dwain Whitson suggests assembling the frame with #18×¾" brads.) To avoid snagging the brads on fabric or marring wood surfaces, glue ½"-wide felt strips around the perimeter.

Sand smooth a 13"-long piece of 1×8 pine (actual dimension: ¾×7½"). (Dwain sands clear white pine with 120-grit sandpaper on his belt sander.) After duplicating the pattern with tracing paper, copy the pattern outline and the dowel centerpoints onto the pine with transfer paper. Test-fit the puzzle in the frame. It will fit looser after cutting out the pieces. Drill ⅜" holes ½" deep for the dowels. (A brad-point bit drills a clean hole.) Then, cut out the puzzle pieces with a ⅛" bandsaw or a No. 5 scrollsaw blade. Sand the cut edges smooth, and retest the fit in the frame.

Cut 10 lengths of ⅜" dowel to 1½" long. Round over one end of each dowel with sandpaper. Then, sand the puzzle parts and frame with 150-grit sandpaper. Remove dust with a tack cloth, and seal the frame, puzzle parts, and dowels with fruitwood stain.

Have fun painting

Copy the design onto the front surface of the puzzle pieces with transfer paper. Use a ½" flat brush for large design areas and a No. 4 round brush for small details.

Dinosaur: Paint the dinosaur head and body TU. Apply White to the eye, mouth, and feet. Paint the spine Black.

Footprints: Using a ½" flat brush, paint the footprints OR. Dip the handle end of a brush in OR, and dot the toes.

Finish with pride

Allow the paint to dry thoroughly. To remove fuzz raised by acrylic paint, lightly sand all surfaces with a paper grocery sack. Remove the dust with a tack cloth. Spray all pieces with a matte-finish varnish. Apply a dot of glue to the flat end of each dowel and lightly tap the dowels into place.

Project Tool List

Tablesaw
Scrollsaw or bandsaw
Portable drill or drill press
  ⅜" bit
Finishing sander

Note: *We built the project with the tools listed. You may be able to substitute other tools or equipment for listed items you don't have. Additional common hand tools and clamps may be required to complete the project.*

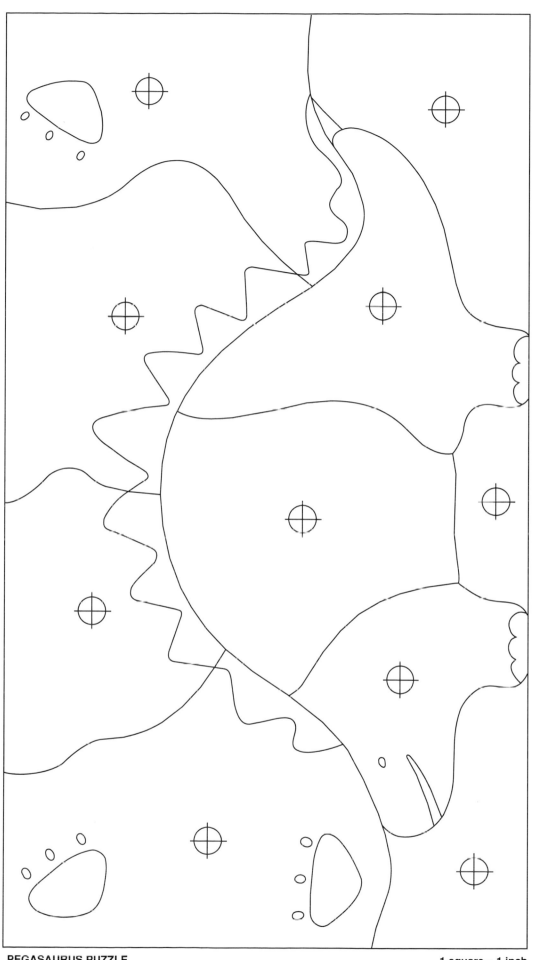

PEGASAURUS PUZZLE

1 square = 1 inch

THE OLD COUNTRY SCHOOLHOUSE

Accept nothing less than an A+ for this gift idea. Any teacher will be proud to display this personalized name plaque on the classroom door.

Start with raw wood

After duplicating the schoolhouse, fence, and sign patterns with tracing paper, copy the schoolhouse outline with transfer paper onto a 13"-long piece of 1×12 pine (actual size: ¾×11¼"). Cut the sign and the seven shaded fence pieces on the pattern from ⅛" pine or plywood. (If your lumberyard or crafts store doesn't carry ⅛" pine, plane or resaw thicker stock to size.) Cut out the pieces with a scrollsaw, using a No. 5 blade.

From ³⁄₁₆" dowel, cut a 1¼" signpost, a 1" swing seat, and a 2⅜" post for the swing stand. From ¼" dowel, cut a 2½" horizontal bar for the swing stand. Drill ³⁄₁₆" and ¼" holes where shown on *page 86*. Sand all surfaces with the grain, using 100- and then 150-grit sandpaper. Remove dust with a tack cloth.

Have fun painting

Thin paints with water 5:1 for base-coating, and about 4:1 (or the consistency of ink) for liner work. Use a No. 12 flat brush to base-coat the grass, roofs, bell tower, bell, and all of the TS areas on the schoolhouse. Use a No. 8 flat brush to base-coat all remaining areas.

Schoolhouse: Do not paint the area underneath the teacher's sign or the signpost. (For good adhesion, always leave an area unpainted so you can glue raw wood to raw wood. Glue will eventually pop if you try to adhere two painted or varnished surfaces.)

Base-coat the door, walls, and bottom of the bell tower TS. Paint the bell tower LI, the bell MG, and the bell tower roof HI with a LI finial. Apply HI to the schoolhouse roof and CG to the step risers. Paint the schoolhouse trim, the window and door frames, the sign over the door, the step treads, and the handrails LI.

Then, using a No. 2 liner brush and Black, add all detail lines on the bell tower and schoolhouse roofs, the siding, and the door. Outline the windows, steps, porch handrails and posts, the sign over the door, and the sign numbers with Black. Dip the handle end of a No. 2 liner brush into LI, and dot the doorknob.

Outbuilding: Paint the roof HI, the building TS, and the door, moon, and latch LI. Then, outline the roof, door details, and the latch with Black. Dot a Black nailhead on the latch.

Landscaping: Base-coat the fence cutouts LI. Paint the fenceposts on the schoolhouse cutout LI, but do not paint the areas that will be under the fence cutouts. Using a stylus or the pointed end of a toothpick, dot Black fence nailheads.

Paint the grass FG, and the flowers ST. Using a No. 2 liner brush, outline the flower petals with RI. Dot flower centers Black. Paint the stepping-stones CG, and outline with Black.

Teacher's sign: Base-coat the front of the sign LI. Paint the edges, the front border, and the personalized lettering Black. Apply SB to three sides of the signpost. Leave the backs of the sign and post unpainted for gluing.

Allow all paint to dry thoroughly. Then, using tacky glue, attach the fence pieces, signpost, and sign where shown on the pattern.

Swing: Thin SB with water 1:1. Using an old rag, stain remaining dowel pieces and the string with this mixture. Wipe off excess paint with a paper towel. Let dowels dry thoroughly.

Finish with pride

Glue the swing stand together where shown on the pattern. Cut the string in half, and tie the seat to the stand. Secure the knots with a drop of glue. Then, lightly sand all pieces smooth with a paper grocery sack. Remove dust with a tack cloth, and finish with two coats of water-based varnish.

Project Tool List

Scrollsaw
Portable drill
  Bits: ³⁄₁₆", ¼"
Finishing sander

Note: We built the project with the tools listed. You may be able to substitute other tools or equipment for listed items you don't have. Additional common hand tools and clamps may be required to complete the project.

continued

Palette

Delta Ceramcoat Colors
  Black
CG   Cadet Gray 2426
FG   Forest Green 2010
HI   Hammered Iron 2094
LI   Light Ivory 2401
RI   Red Iron Oxide 2020
SB   Spice Brown 2049

ST   Straw 2078
TS   Tomato Spice 2098
Delta Metallics
MG   Metallic Gold

Brushes

No. 12 synthetic flat
No. 8 synthetic flat
No. 2 synthetic liner

Supplies

1×12×13" pine
⅛×1×22" pine or Baltic birch
  plywood
³⁄₁₆×5" dowel
¼×2⅝" dowel
Tacky glue
6" of string
Water-based varnish

THE OLD COUNTRY SCHOOLHOUSE
continued

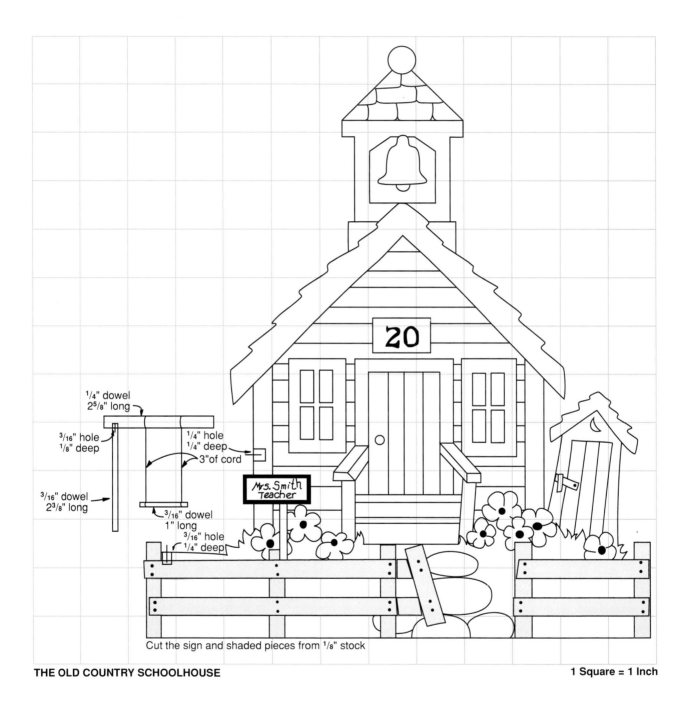

¹/₄" dowel 2⁵/₈" long

³/₁₆" hole ¹/₈" deep

¹/₄" hole ¹/₄" deep
3"of cord

³/₁₆" dowel 2³/₈" long

³/₁₆" dowel 1" long
³/₁₆" hole ¹/₄" deep

Mrs. Smith Teacher

20

Cut the sign and shaded pieces from ¹/₈" stock

THE OLD COUNTRY SCHOOLHOUSE

1 Square = 1 Inch

JUGGLES THE CLOWN

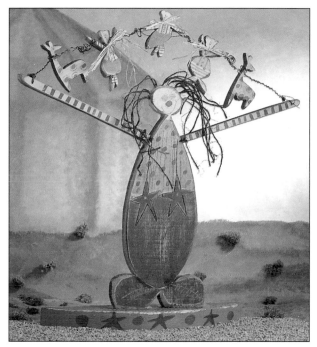

S tep right up to the wildest, wackiest crafting experience we've had the opportunity to bring to you. If your own life is a three-ring circus at times, having Juggles around will bring smiles from the whole family.

Start with raw wood

Duplicate the clown patterns with tracing paper. Copy the clown outlines with transfer paper onto 1" pine (actual thickness: ¾"), the base outline onto 2" pine (actual thickness: 1½"), and the giraffes and bears outlines onto ½" pine. (If your lumberyard doesn't carry ½" pine, plane or resaw thicker stock to size.)

Cut out the pieces with a scroll-saw, using a No. 5 blade for the clown, giraffes, and bears, and a No. 9 blade for the base. Drill ⅛" and ¼" holes where shown on the patterns.

Sand with the grain, using 100- and then 150-grit sandpaper. Remove dust with a tack cloth. Copy pattern details onto the cutouts with transfer paper. Define the suspenders, suspender stars, and shoelaces by carving out a

V-groove. (Project designer Linda Williams uses a No. 5 X-ACTO carver's knife fitted with a ½" flat blade.)

Have fun painting

Thin all paints with water 5:1. Base-coat all areas with a 1" sponge brush. Paint stars and dots with a No. 4 round brush, and paint stripes with a ⅛" flat brush. Do not apply heavy coverage, since you will be sanding the painted surfaces after the paint dries.

Clown: Base-coat the pants front IN, and the shirt front HC. Apply AS to the shoe fronts and edges, the body edges, and the suspender stars. Paint the suspenders and half of the shirt dots IN. Paint the remaining shirt dots AS.

Base-coat the arm fronts and the face TA. Paint the arm edges, arm stripes, and nose AS, and paint the eye circles BP.

Then, using a crafts knife, score lines around the eyes, nose, and both vertically and horizontally on the shirt front. Leave ½" between each scored shirt line. (Linda says the lines add texture. You really have to look to see them. But, she feels that they enhance the primitive style she favors.)

With a black marking pen, outline the shirt dots, and draw the vertical stripes and small stars on the shirt front. Make "+" markings in each eye, and add the mouth.

Clown's base: Base-coat the front edge EM and the top IN. Do not paint the areas where you adhere the clown's feet. (For good adhesion, always glue or epoxy bare wood to bare wood. Glue or epoxy eventually pops if you

adhere two painted or varnished surfaces.) Paint AS stars and TB circles. Then, using a crafts knife, score lines around dots and stars.

Giraffes: Base-coat the giraffe fronts TA. Paint the spots AS. Outline the spots and draw the eyes with a permanent black marking pen.

Dancing bears: Base-coat the fronts TA, and the edges AS. Referring to the photograph at *left,* paint clothes with AS, EM, and TB. With a black marking pen, outline the buttons, draw button stars, and add the faces.

Finish with pride

Using 100-grit sandpaper, lightly sand some paint off the front of each piece. Then, sand the edges, removing most of the paint.

Wipe the edges and backs of all pieces with a medium-walnut stain. Allow the stain to dry thoroughly. Lightly sand with a paper grocery sack, and remove dust with a tack cloth. Then, spray all surfaces with a satin-finish varnish.

Cut jute into 8 pieces, each 16" long. Paint the jute AS. Double each strand, and use epoxy to secure jute into each hole in the head. Attach the clown to the base with 1⅞"-long dowels and epoxy.

Using 20-gauge black wire and referring to the photograph *above left* fasten the arms to the body and the animals to the arms. Tie raffia bows around each bear's neck.

Project Tool List
Scrollsaw
Portable drill
  Bits: ⅛", ¼"
Finishing sander

Note: We built the project with the tools listed. You may be able to substitute other tools or equipment for listed items you don't have. Additional common hand tools and clamps may be required to complete the project.

continued

JUGGLES THE CLOWN
continued

Palette

FolkArt Colors
- AS Apple Spice 951
- BP Butter Pecan 939
- EM English Mustard 959
- HC Honeycomb 942
- IN Indigo 908
- TA Tapioca 903
- TB Thunder Blue 609

Brushes

1" sponge
No. 4 synthetic round
⅛" synthetic flat

Supplies

1x8x16" pine
2x4x16" pine
½x4x24" pine
¼x4" dowel
Medium-tipped permanent black marking pen
5-minute epoxy
3 yards of No. 20-gauge black wire
4 yards of thin-ply jute
Carver's straight chisel
X-ACTO knife or crafts knife
1 yard of raffia
Medium-walnut stain
Satin-finish spray varnish

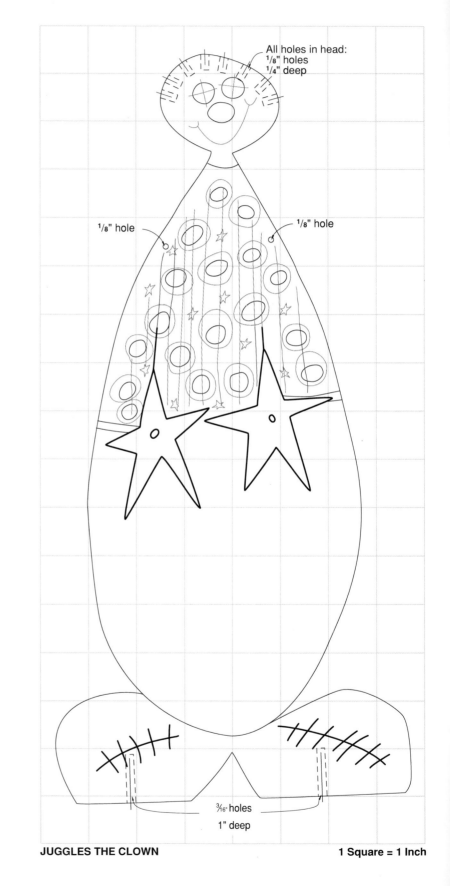

All holes in head: ⅛" holes ¼" deep

⅛" hole

⅛" hole

³⁄₁₆" holes 1" deep

JUGGLES THE CLOWN

1 Square = 1 Inch

JUGGLES THE CLOWN

1 Square = 1 Inch

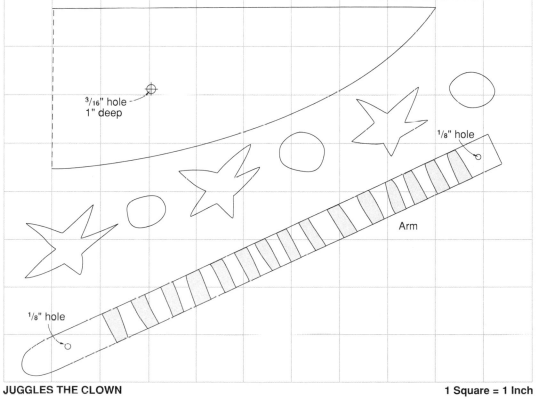

$^3/_{16}$" hole
1" deep

$^1/_8$" hole

$^1/_8$" hole

Arm

$^1/_8$" hole

JUGGLES THE CLOWN

1 Square = 1 Inch

A FANCIFUL FENCE FULL OF BUNNIES

Hop right up to your work surface and craft a bunch of these adorable bunnies for your mantel or holiday table. Screen molding is the secret ingredient in our easy-to-build fence.

Start with raw wood

After duplicating the patterns with tracing paper, copy the outlines with transfer paper onto ¼"-thick pine or poplar. (If your lumberyard doesn't carry ¼" pine, plane or resaw thicker stock to size.). We resawed 1" pine to ¼". Cut out the rabbits, birds, carrots, and hearts with a scrollsaw, using a No. 5 blade. Sand with the grain, using 100- and then 150-grit sandpaper. Remove the dust with a tack cloth.

Cut the screen molding into eight 12½" lengths for the fence rails. Cut 24 pickets 3½" long. Then, cut a point on each picket top. Drill holes about ⁵⁄₁₆" in from each rail end, using a ³⁄₁₆" drill bit. Using woodworker's glue, assemble the pickets and fence rails. (Refer to the fence pattern on *page 92.*)

Have fun painting

Thin all paints with water 5:1, and base-coat the fence and the individual pieces, following the directions *below.*

Fence: Using the 1" flat brush, paint the four fence sections White. After the paint dries, sand lightly with 150-grit sandpaper.

Bunnies: Base-coat all four bunnies White. After the paint dries, sand lightly. Then, transfer the details onto the bunny cutouts with tracing paper.

With a ¼" flat brush, paint the coveralls CC and the dresses CA. Paint the clothing on the front, back, and edges of the bunny cutouts. Dip the handle end of a brush into Black, and dot the eyes. Using the liner brush, paint the eyebrows Black and the nose and mouth CA. Dip a cotton swab in CA and rub off most of the paint on the swab with a

Palette	Supplies
Delta Ceramcoat Colors	¼x4x32" white pine or
AD Adriatic 02438	yellow poplar
Black 02506	16 feet of screen molding
CA Cayenne 02428	Cotton swab
CC Cape Cod 02133	¼"-wide V-groove carving tool
White 02505	or X-ACTO knife
	5-minute epoxy
Brushes	Blue embroidery floss
¼" synthetic flat	8" of 19-gauge black wire
1" synthetic flat	No. 55 drill bit
No. 0 synthetic liner	1 package of green raffia
Toothbrush or spatter brush	Matte-finish spray varnish
	3x3" fabric scrap for bows

FULL-SIZED PATTERNS

Cut 2

¹/₁₆" hole

Cut 2

paper towel. Then, blush the cheeks and the inside of the ears with the swab. Using the liner brush and Black, paint whiskers on each side of the bunny's nose. Paint CC checks on the dress bottoms, CA buttons on the coveralls, and dashed Black lines along the ends of the coverall shoulder straps.

With a ¼" V-groove carving tool or X-ACTO knife, gouge a groove from the feet upward to separate the legs.

Birds and hearts: Apply a base coat of AD to the birds and CC to

the hearts. Sand lightly. Using a ¼" V-groove carving tool or knife, cut a shallow semicircular groove for the wing on both sides of the birds. With the handle end of a brush, dot Black eyes on both sides of the birds. Using a No. 55 drill bit (available at hardware stores), make a ½"-deep hole for each wire bird leg. Make two holes in the fence rail where the feet attach. Cut four 2" pieces of wire, and epoxy the wire into the holes in the bird. Allow the epoxy to set. Then, bend the wire to form the legs.

Carrots: Base-coat the carrots CA. Sand lightly. Using a ⅛" drill bit, drill a hole ½" deep into the top for the carrot greens. Epoxy strands of green raffia into the holes. Let the epoxy set.

Finish with pride

Epoxy a carrot to each boy rabbit's left hand. Then, epoxy the boy rabbits to the fence. Drill a ¹/₁₆" hole in each girl rabbit's right hand and in one top corner of each heart. Attach the heart, using all six
continued

A FANCIFUL FENCE FULL OF BUNNIES
continued

strands of embroidery floss and a square knot. Epoxy the girl rabbits to the fence. Then epoxy the wire bird legs into the fence. With an old toothbrush or spatter brush, lightly spatter both sides of the fence sections with Black. When the paint dries, spray both sides with clear varnish.

Cut 8" lengths of floss, and tie a bow at each girl's neck. Make two small bow ties from a fabric scrap, and glue one in place at each boy rabbit's neck.

Tie the fence sections together with bows, using three 20"-long pieces of raffia at each joint. Trim bows to desired length.

Project Tool List
Tablesaw
Scrollsaw
Portable drill or drill press
    Bits: No. 55, ⅟₁₆", ⅛", ³⁄₁₆"
Finishing sander

Note: *We built the project with the tools listed. You may be able to substitute other tools or equipment for listed items you don't have. Additional common hand tools and clamps may be required to complete the project.*

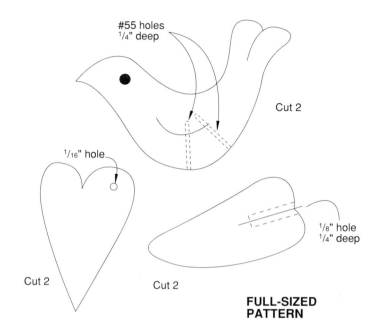

#55 holes ¼" deep

Cut 2

⅟₁₆" hole

⅛" hole ¼" deep

Cut 2

Cut 2

FULL-SIZED PATTERN

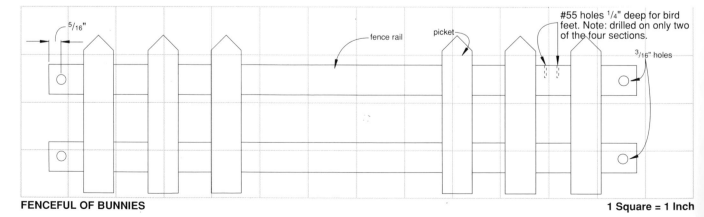

5/16"

fence rail

picket

#55 holes ¼" deep for bird feet. Note: drilled on only two of the four sections.

³⁄₁₆" holes

FENCEFUL OF BUNNIES

1 Square = 1 Inch

MOOO-NLIGHT FUN

Cow: Paint all surfaces WW. Then, transfer the spots onto the front and back of the cow with transfer paper. Paint the spots LI. Wrap the spots around the edges to add dimension. Project designer Quink Arlt suggests painting the front and the edges first, and then connecting them smoothly with the spots on the back.

Moon: Paint the moon BC. With a liner brush, paint the mouth and eyes AB.

Trees: Apply TH to all surfaces of the trees. Allow the pieces to dry.

Using 100-grit sandpaper, lightly sand paint off the front and back of the trees, cow, and moon. Then, sand the edges to remove even more paint.

Finish with pride

Wipe all surfaces of the trees, moon, base, cow, and dowels with a medium-walnut oil stain. Allow the stain to dry thoroughly.

To remove fuzz raised by acrylic paints, lightly sand with a paper grocery sack. Remove dust with a tack cloth. Then, spray all surfaces with a satin-finish spray varnish.

continued

Palette

FolkArt Colors

AB	Acorn Brown 941
BC	Buttercup 905
LI	Licorice 938
TH	Thicket 924
WW	Wicker White 901

Brushes

1" synthetic flat
¼" synthetic flat
No. 00 synthetic liner

Supplies

1x2x12½" pine
1x6x30" pine
¼x12" dowel
4" of jute
Medium-walnut oil stain
Satin-finish spray varnish

Under starry skies like these, you won't be able to fence in this Holstein. Beginners and youngsters alike will find this project udderly delightful. And, because it's quick to complete, it's a winner for church bazaars.

Start with raw wood

After duplicating the patterns with tracing paper, copy the outlines with transfer paper onto a 30"-long piece of 1x6 clear white pine (actual size: ¾x5½"). Cut out the six pieces with a scrollsaw,

using a No. 5 blade. Next, sand with the grain, using 100- and then 150-grit sandpaper. Remove the dust with a tack cloth.

Cut three 3"-long pieces of ¼"-diameter dowel for the tree trunks. Cut two ¾"-long pieces from the ¼"-diameter dowel.

Have fun painting

Use a 1" flat brush to paint large areas, a ¼" flat brush to fill in the cow's spots, and a liner brush for the mouth and eyes on the moon. Dilute paints with water 5:1.

MOOO-NLIGHT FUN
continued

Before drilling any holes, Quink suggests that you lay the painted pieces together on a flat surface. Refer to the photograph on *page 93* for positioning. Put a drop of paint on the cow's tummy and on the top of the smallest tree. As you reposition the pieces, these dots will leave a mark on the cutouts precisely where you want to drill dowel holes.

Drill a ¼" hole ½" deep in the bottom center of each tree and in the rear of the cow for the tail. Drill three ¼" holes in the rectangular base, referring to the pattern for placement. With a ¼" drill bit, make a hole in the tummy of the cow, the top and bottom of the moon, and the top of the smallest tree.

Place a drop of yellow woodworkers' glue in each hole in the base. Insert a 3"-long dowel into each hole, and push firmly in place. Then, glue one tree to each tree trunk, with the smallest tree in the center.

Glue the jute into the tail opening. Then, unravel the jute tail. Using the small pieces of ⅛" dowel, glue the moon to the top of the center tree. Then, glue the cow to the moon.

Project Tool List
Scrollsaw
Portable drill
    ¼" bit
Finishing sander

Note: *We built the project with the tools listed. You may be able to substitute other tools or equipment for listed items you don't have. Additional common hand tools and clamps may be required to complete the project.*

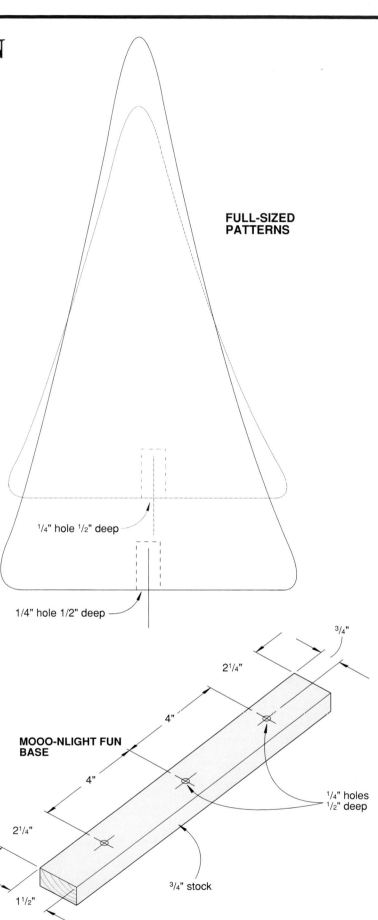

FULL-SIZED PATTERNS

¼" hole ½" deep

1/4" hole 1/2" deep

3/4"

2¼"

4"

MOOO-NLIGHT FUN BASE

4"

¼" holes ½" deep

2¼"

3/4" stock

1½"